EVES AGAINST THE ODDS
25 INSPIRING WOMEN ENTREPRENEURS STORIES

CURATED BY
BHAVESH KOTHARI
HARIHARAN IYER

INDIA · SINGAPORE · MALAYSIA

Notion Press Media Pvt Ltd

No. 50, Chettiyar Agaram Main Road,
Vanagaram, Chennai, Tamil Nadu – 600 095

First Published by Notion Press 2021
Copyright © Billennium Divas Private Limited 2021
All Rights Reserved.

ISBN 978-1-63997-559-4

This book has been published with all efforts taken to make the material error-free after the consent of the author. However, the author and the publisher do not assume and hereby disclaim any liability to any party for any loss, damage, or disruption caused by errors or omissions, whether such errors or omissions result from negligence, accident, or any other cause.

While every effort has been made to avoid any mistake or omission, this publication is being sold on the condition and understanding that neither the author nor the publishers or printers would be liable in any manner to any person by reason of any mistake or omission in this publication or for any action taken or omitted to be taken or advice rendered or accepted on the basis of this work. For any defect in printing or binding the publishers will be liable only to replace the defective copy by another copy of this work then available.

Dedicated To

Bhavesh's mother Late Smt. Chandrika Jayant Kothari
&
To all the women entrepreneurs out there who battle the odds everyday to come out triumphant.

Bhavesh's Note For His Mother

This book is Dedicated to **'My Billennium Diva'**: My Mother, Late Smt. Chandrika Jayant Kothari (Champavanti Hiralal Parekh). A true diva in her own self, a doting daughter, a loving and caring wife and the most beautiful mother, a friend, a true "Women Power", a warrior queen and most important, a wonderful human being who embraced and fought countless battles and came victorious. She was an epitome of selflessness, love, kindness, humility and warmth who nurtured the family and made sure she upheld and instilled a value system in all of us.

It is difficult and daunting to bind two different families together, and she did that with such swiftness, charm and smile. She played innumerable roles not only in our lives, but for many others too. She hailed from a rich and well-educated Gujarati family, which migrated to India from Aden and settled in Mumbai. She was the sixth child amongst the eight brothers and sisters, but was the most loved amongst all the siblings.

After marriage, she handled all problems, including financial, with great grace and dignity. She made sure that her three children were given the best of everything, including the essential moral values. Her journey from life's comforts to hardships to comforts is an inspiration not only for the family, but also to many others who knew her. Though a homemaker, she had an entrepreneurial spirit in her.

Words fall short to describe my mother's greatness.

As Rudyard Kipling said: "God could not be everywhere, and therefore he made mothers."

She is My True Diva, and I am blessed to be her son. This is for you Mummy!

25 Inspiring Women Entrepreneurs:

- Ms. Pabiben Rabari
- Dr. Tarita Shankar
- Dr. Ushy Mohan Das
- Ms. Nabomita Mazumdar
- Ms. Sharmila Divatia
- Ms. Shabia Walia
- Ms. Manisha Raisinghani
- Ms. Jaya Vaidhyanathan
- Ms. Reema Sanghavi
- Ms. Tanul Mishra
- Ms. Neha Kanabar
- Ms. Shikha Pandey
- Ms. Shridaa Raheja
- Ms. Namrata Tatiya
- Ms. Chandni Khan
- Ms. Neety Gupta
- Ms. Namita Shah
- Dr. Sandhya Mayenkar
- Ms. Vinika Chandwani
- Dr. Anubha Singhai
- Ms. Ivy Manohara
- Ms. Suvarna Bhat
- Dr. Megha Bhatt
- Ms. Roli Pandey
- Dr. Tejal Kanwar

CONTENTS

Foreword..9
Preface..11
Salute to Women Entrepreneurs...............13
Special Write-Up................................15
Special Note.....................................19

25 INSPIRING STORIES OF WOMEN ENTREPRENEURS

1. Ms. Pabiben Rabari..........................22
2. Dr. Tarita Shankar...........................26
3. Dr. Ushy Mohan Das........................30
4. Ms. Nabomita Mazumdar...................34
5. Ms. Sharmila Divatia........................38
6. Ms. Shabia Walia............................42
7. Ms. Manisha Raisinghani..................46
8. Ms. Jaya Vaidhyanathan....................50
9. Ms. Reema Sanghavi.......................54
10. Ms. Tanul Mishra...........................58
11. Ms. Neha Kanabar..........................64
12. Ms. Shikha Pandey.........................68

13. Ms. Shridaa Raheja 72

14. Ms. Namrata Tatiya 76

15. Ms. Chandni Khan 80

16. Ms. Neety Gupta 84

17. Ms. Namita Shah 88

18. Dr. Sandhya Mayenkar 92

19. Ms. Vinika Chandwani 96

20. Dr. Anubha Singhai 100

21. Ms. Ivy Manohara 104

22. Ms. Suvarna Bhat 110

23. Dr. Megha Bhatt 114

24. Ms. Roli Pandey 118

25. Dr. Tejal Kanwar 124

About the Authors *129*

FOREWORD

I am delighted to write the foreword for this book, not just because it is about women entrepreneurs by women entrepreneurs, but also because it has been compiled by two conscientious gentlemen. We certainly need more such empowered men to come forward and lead the way for women entrepreneurs to grow and excel.

The post Covid-19 world has changed the way we live. Many men experienced lockdown for the first time, but homemakers for so many decades have made this world a better place by staying indoors. Besides, many women professionals as well as entrepreneurs are still fundamentally rooted to the role of managing house work, as it is simply in our genes.

The Super Woman now needs to dig into her inner reserves even more as the world has dramatically changed in just a few months. We will probably never live the way we lived till quite recently. I strongly believe women can show the way, as they have one quality in abundance which is most required now – Resilience.

Each story in this book is unique and captures the inspiring journey of each entrepreneur lucidly. Each person's experience is different. However, the two elements I feel common to all the storytellers are Enterprise and The Ability To Do The Balancing Act. The new world we find ourselves now is a result of not respecting nature enough and getting carried away by greed. We need to restore balance between man and nature, transactions and relationships, and family and work. This is complex, but women are masters at managing complexity.

We are now facing a new dimension of complexity. As bureaucrats, we too have to handle a wide range of complexities, so that we can keep in balance the various forces that make a nation. We in government want to do everything possible to encourage enterprising women to take up entrepreneurship and bring about a social change through their business model. I congratulate The

Billennium Divas for their work. We are delighted to partner with them in their vision to make India stronger by making women stronger.

Heartiest congratulations to all the Women Entrepreneurs who have been shortlisted to contribute for this inspiring book. I feel more inspired after reading the stories and I am sure the readers will feel the same. More power to all of you.

With Best Wishes to team Billennium Divas.

By Ms. Anju Sharma, IAS
Principal Secretary (Higher & Technical Education),
Education Department, Government of Gujarat.

PREFACE

This is a labour of love from Team Billennium Divas (BDF). Curating some of the most inspiring stories of women entrepreneurs provided us with great moments of joy. Each story inspires you to inspire. We believe no story lives unless someone wants to listen and we at BDF want everyone to 'listen' through this book. We hope by going through these pages many women will feel inspired enough either to take to entrepreneurship or take their business journey to the next level. After all, the stories we love best do live in us forever.

These stories are intricately and carefully woven together, and thus they became a part of the Top

"25 Inspiring Women Entrepreneurs" who have moved boulders with their grit, determination, confidence, chased their dreams and fought all odds and are ready to take on the world. BDF has brought out this book to honour excellence and celebrate the spirit of entrepreneurship.

Women Power: "Unleash the power within you"!

This book would not have been possible without the support of the 25 storytellers and few other important people. But before that, an important note for the readers. *The writers have shared their stories in different formats – like first person or third person. We have simply done some editing and tried to retain the essence and spirit of their stories.*

Our sincere thanks to:

- Ms. Anju Sharma, IAS for her thought-provoking foreword.
- Ms. Shweta Shalini for her insights and setting the tone for the book through her own story and for her constant support and motivation to Billennium Divas.
- Shri. Ashish Chauhan - Managing Director and Chief Executive Officer, Bombay Stock Exchange for his invaluable support.

- Shri. Khushro Bulsara, Head – IPF, BSE Investor Protection Fund
- And to BSE Investor Protection Fund for their wholehearted support to our sincere initiative.

Special Thanks to Dr. Kiran Bedi, IAS, a legend everyone looks up to. Her words are timeless and inspiring.

Big Gratitude to Ms. Minal Kothari – Co-Founder & Director, Billennium Divas. Thanks to our team: Mr. Tapaswi Patel, Mr. Pratik Lalani, Mr. Purvang Joshi and our Dynamic Evangelist Divas – Ms. Shweta Shalini, Ms. Rajashri Rajashekhar, Ms. Nabomita Mazumdar, Rtn. Alpa Shah, Ms. Shoma Mittra, Ms. Deepika Singh, Ms. Shubhangi Mitra, Ms. Aparna Mishra, and to all the Member Divas of Billennium Divas and all the divas out there.

We also wish to thank Pratik Lalani for the wonderful cover design.

A Big thank you to Notion Press for publishing this book.

By Bhavesh Kothari & Hariharan Iyer

SALUTE TO WOMEN ENTREPRENEURS

It is indeed a great pleasure to share my thoughts for this wonderful book by the Billennium Divas aptly titled as "Eves Against The Odds" – 25 Inspiring Women Entrepreneurs Stories.

I have been in public service for so long and have come across many amazing people across the world. I have also had the opportunity to meet people from various walks of life across India. Every time I feel it can't get more amazing than this person, another one comes along. That's what India is – a constantly flowing stream of talent and ability.

Resilience is at the core of Indian life. Who better represents this than women? The silent and selfless homemakers, working professionals and women entrepreneurs, they all keep this nation chugging along with a daily dose of optimism and courage.

The one thing our country needs is for enterprising women to stand up and be counted. What better way to do that than through entrepreneurship? I can see that the Billennium Divas community is taking initiatives that can propel the spirit of enterprise in women. It is a platform for those who seek it to grow self and the people they work with.

I congratulate Billennium Divas for coming up with these fantastic stories of eves who continuously fight against the odds and make this country proud through their business idea and execution. My heartiest congratulations and thanks to the 25 women entrepreneurs for sharing their inspiring stories for the larger public good. I am sure Billennium Divas will continue to provide such wonderful opportunities for women entrepreneurs.

Women, as you know, need just this one thing – Encouragement, and Billennium Divas provides loads of it. Congratulations and best wishes to the whole community and those who are a part of it in some way or the other.

My best wishes to all of you at Team Billennium Divas.

By Dr. Kiran Bedi, IAS
Former Lt. Governor of Puducherry,
Founder - Navjyoti India Foundation and India Vision Foundation.

SPECIAL WRITE-UP

I wanted to make this write-up different because I am different and so is every single woman in this book. Unlike all the Inspiring Women Entrepreneur books that you would have seen, this compilation is different too…

So, here I list 12 Interesting facts about me That many don't know but you should… if you want to be an entrepreneur.

1. I am a Billennium Diva!

I was always told that women come together to gossip and I was determined to set up a platform where they can come together to grow mentally, emotionally and financially.

This is each for equal is action.

2. I hail from a small village & married into one

I hail from a small village called Binda in Muzaffarpur in Bihar. It's famous for lichis. I got married into a small village called Amsin in Ayodhya, based on the bank of river Saryu.

I am proud of my roots, my upbringing and that helped me be grounded.

3. I had a Nomadic Childhood

I have studied in 9 different schools in nearly 5 different states because my father was an Army Officer. Changing culture, times and situations built my character. Hence, I am Shweta adaptable Shalini.

4. My name has a HISTORY

My father was active in the JP Movement and he was against the caste system. He believed that a Man/Woman should be known by his Name (which he or she makes with his work) and not by his surname. So he dropped his Surname and named both his Children with Names Creative enough to NOT have a Surname.

Hence, MY name is *Shweta Shalini*

5. I Sing well (at least I claim so…)

I started singing in Sunder Kand mandalis at the age of 12 years and also used to win in Antaksharis during my College days.

I sing when I'm happy, I sing when I'm lonely and sing when I'm stressed. Post which I am my usual self-smiling & confident.

6. I am a Mechanical Engineer

Yes. I am, I am proud of it… I also worked for a Mechanical Engineering company… but now I have multiple IT start-ups.

I challenge the usual & accept the exceptional.

7. I was the first Woman Employee in Sales & Marketing in Atlas Copco, India

I nearly gave half a dozen interviews and realized that they were looking at experimenting with me to see if girls could work in a mechanical company and in Sales.

Now, they have a few hundred women. So, a leader is usually lonely but she sets the trend.

8. I failed in my First Start-Up

I started a trading company and learnt what not to do and hence in all my future ventures I was successful.

The key was a consistent belief that if anyone could ever do it, it was me!

9. I started my Company when I was pregnant with Twins!

So, I thought to myself that God had blessed me with Triplets (two kids & one startup) and I had to be fair and just to all three.

Now I have multiple Ventures - all in the field of Tech & IT.

10. I believe in LOVE

I married my best friend; he still is my best friend. I Love my life, love my work, love my country, love Modi ji & Love my ethics.

Try Love, it can make Impossible possible.

11. I write Shayaris…

I used to write stories, proses, poems, songs & a lot of shayari all throughout my student life… Now, it's usually social media, especially for you people.

किताबों में जो लिखा नहीं था…
सिखाया वो सबक़ हमें ज़िंदगी ने!!

12. I have NO-ONE in Politics

I am a self-made person. When I started Entrepreneurship, I was the first in my family to do so.

Today, I am a complete OUTLIER in Politics, with no one to support or hand hold. I am trying to make a mark in a world filled with biases, casteism, gender inequality ONLY based on my hard work, competence & differentiation… And guess what, I have been supported, generously showered with love and appreciated.

I believe that the time for Women Entrepreneurship is now.

I had my share of struggles & we all do. Throughout the book you will read Women stories of grit, commitment and persistence. But the time for the India Growth story and the contribution of the Woman workforce will start now.

While competing with China, one advantage we always had was English. Now onwards the advantage will be the rising Women workforce in all sectors, all geographies and all skill levels.

Women will have their Way.

By Ms. Shweta Shalini
Entrepreneur, TEDx Speaker,
Executive Director - Maharashtra Village Social Transformation Foundation, Advisor to Ex CM, GoM

SPECIAL NOTE

I am delighted to share my thoughts for this unique book by the Billennium Divas aptly titled as Eves Against The Odds – 25 Inspiring Women Entrepreneurs Stories.

Everyday people watch the Sensex. Everyday India also watches and learns from the enterprising spirit of its women folks. India cannot find its rightful place in the world if all its people don't get involved and inspired to contribute in all spheres. Women will play a special role in these endeavours.

Billennium Divas is show-casing women leaders through this book to inspire people to emulate the champions. It has been engaged in encouraging and nurturing women entrepreneurs in other ways too.

My best wishes to all of you at Team Billennium Divas.

By Shri. Ashish Chauhan
Managing Director and Chief Executive Officer,
Bombay Stock Exchange.

* * *

About BSE Investors Protection Fund (BSE IPF)

"BSE Investors Protection Fund (BSE IPF) was established in 1986 as an Approved Charitable Trust, under the mandate of the Ministry of Finance. The IPF Secretariat was set up in 2010 with the objective of spreading financial awareness and literacy, to meet claims of clients against defaulting BSE brokers, arrange IAPs throughout the country in association with Investors' Associations registered with SEBI. Educational Institutions, SEBI, professional bodies like ICSI, ICAI organize events and conferences in association with local Chambers of Commerce and Industry for Investor Awareness and Education and to educate the investors on various products available in the capital markets."

"Eves Against The Odds" – 25 Inspiring Women Entrepreneurs Stories by Billennium Divas is a unique and standout initiative which is launched during the Women Power Summit & Awards 2021 that honours the strength, creativity, courage and resourcefulness of Women. The true contribution by Women in Society is never fully acknowledged or appreciated. This pandemic has made us witness these miracle workers like homemakers who juggle so many roles effortlessly day in and day out and it is only now that we really see their work for what it is. BSE IPF is proud to associate with this wonderful initiative and honour them. We believe that Financial Awareness and Education will empower more women to fly even higher and reach newer heights! Thank you."

Mr. Khushro Bulsara
Head - IPF
BSE Investor Protection Fund.

25 INSPIRING STORIES OF WOMEN ENTREPRENEURS

MS. PABIBEN
RABARI

FOUNDER
PABIBEN.COM

About Ms. Pabiben Rabari

Pabiben, a vibrant Rabari lady, struggled in her childhood and got fame at a young age. She dared to start one of the first women artisan enterprises, pabiben.com. Pabiben was born in Kukadsar village of Mundra taluka in Kutch. She could not attend school, as her mother Tejuben, a young widow, needed help with raising three girls. The eldest, Pabiben, cared for her sisters. Pabiben learnt the famed embroidery of her community.

Pabiben, along with other Dhebaria women, searched for a way to solve their design problem: how to remain decorative without breaking the community rules. They invented a new art form: machine application of readymade elements, which they called "Hari Jari". For the first time in the Dhebaria community, Pabiben used a vibrant combination of trims and ribbons. Later it came to be known as "Pabi Jari". She has become an inspiration and idol to many in her community.

MY STORY

Why I became an entrepreneur?

I worked many years for Traders, NGOs and Designers, but no one was ready to give me credit. Most businesses work with artisans, develop their own brand and there is no major change in the life of an artisan. Artisan labour and get wages for that. They never get Identity, Value and Recognition. To give Identity, Value and Recognition to the artisans, I started the first women artisan brand Pabiben.com

What is the mission of my business?

We have developed a successful model for rural women. Those who want to become an entrepreneur will face the same problems which Pabiben did. To resolve these problems, we have initiated Kaarigar Clinic, a rural business clinic for artisans. Our mission is to create strong and sustainable business for Kaarigars, who are very keen to develop their own business, but unable to do so due to lack of education, resources, business, management and design skills.

We want to develop 1,000 women entrepreneurs across rural India and create livelihood for 1,00,000 families.

My failures and successes.

Failures

1. When we decided on our brand "Pabiben.com" and put our label on each of our products, few of our buyers opposed and returned our products, causing huge financial loss.
2. When I started my business, I lost my mother-in law on the first day of my first exhibition. We had prepared a huge inventory of my latest collection. But I had to cancel that exhibition and return home.

Successes

1. We were advocating for artisan identity, value and recognition. So we decided my name as our brand name, which was a great decision and brought great success.
2. During lockdown, we initiated the concept of local gift box, which was a great success and were invited by Kaun Banega Crorepati.

What I learnt from my failures

Beyond a point one needs to follow one's own trajectory without bothering too much about what people say.

My advice to Startups

The one thing that has stood me in good stead along my journey is that I never thought of giving up, no matter how hard the circumstances.

My advice to Women entrepreneurs

My advice to other women who want to become entrepreneurs is to never accept defeat. Every one of us experiences struggles and obstacles. As long as you remain steadfast in your purpose, you are bound to eventually find success.

I feel support from home is important for women to make a success in their careers.

My Success Mantra: The real empowerment is the ability to think and choose. Use maximum creativity in our work, match the potential in ourselves to fulfil our dreams and get self-respect and recognition.

Achievements

1. Yashraj banner made a film "Sui Dhaga Heroes Made in India" on pabiben, which was launched before the official launching of sui dhaga.
2. Pabiben made 4 logos for Bollywood film Sui dhaga.
3. Pabiben's success story has been selected for a Digital India campaign "Pragati Yatra", one year achievement of Narendra Modi Government.
4. Facebook made a documentary film on Pabiben
5. Republic TV telecast a special episode "Facebook One India" on pabiben.
6. DD National telecast special interview of pabiben for womenia.
7. State Bank of India made an advertisement on Pabiben
8. Franklin Templeton made an advertisement on Pabiben
9. Reliance Jio and Cisco made 4G advertisement on Pabiben.
10. CNBC telecast a special programme 'Changing India' on Pabiben.
11. Pabiben has been chosen as official brand ambassador for Election Commission Of India.
12. Pabiben has been invited as a Karmaveer in "Kaun Banega Crorepati"

Awards

1. Best Rural Entrepreneur by Ministry of MSME, Govt. of India, by Hon. Minister Kalraj Mishra
2. Jankidevi Bajaj Puraskar for Gandhian Rural Business Model by Jamnalal Bajaj Foundation
3. My FM Jiyo Dil se Award by FM radio
4. NABARD Excellence in Business Initiative Award
5. Prerna Award for Digital Innovation in rural India by Schneider Electric, France
6. Nari Shakti Award by Gujarat Government.
7. Mahila Shakti Award by ASSOCHAM
8. Women of the Year Award by FICCI 2019, by Sushmita Sen
9. International Craft Award 2019 during India Craft Week
10. Smriti Chihna award by Hon.CM, Vijay Rupani, Gujarat Government.
11. Citation by Gurjari, Government of Gujarat

DR. TARITA SHANKAR

CHAIRPERSON
INDIRA GROUP OF INSTITUTES, PUNE.

FOUNDER
SECRETARY & CHIEF MANAGING TRUSTEE - SHREE CHANAKYA EDUCATION SOCIETY.

About Dr. Tarita Shankar

Dr. Tarita Shankar's meteoric rise from a young family-oriented girl to an exemplary leader was paved with several hurdles, personal and professional challenges. She overcame these through pure grit and determination, ability to adapt to changes and an unending quest for excellence. An avid reader, an excellent orator renowned for her free, frank and fearless expression of her views, she loves to travel, having visited all major countries over the world. Philanthropy and concern for the less fortunate occupies her leisure time. Above all, she's a doting mother, an affectionate family woman, and a fun loving, down to earth personality.

HER STORY

For the past twenty-five years, the person who has been continuously and untiringly working in the field of education and social work is none other than the Indira Group of Institutes Chairperson, Dr. Tarita Shankar. At the age of 13, Dr. Tarita played the role of Indian Prime Minister Smt. Indira Gandhi in a play and also won a prize for her performance.

Emboldened by that role, she started an educational institution in the year 1994, taking up space on lease, and in the last twenty-five years, it has transformed as a leading Institution not only in Pune but across the country. It is through this organization that Dr. Tarita could be a source of inspiration and encouragement to many.

Of course, her journey was not at all easy. During the year 1990, when the winds of privatization and the free economy started flowing into India, the doors of many new businesses were opened. At the same time, Dr. Tarita Shankar decided to take a leap in the field of education, with the intention of doing something good in this field. After making her debut in the field of education in 1994, there was no looking back.

Her built-in qualities of being a workaholic, passion for innovation, hard work, her extraordinary foresightedness and collaborative attitude of taking everyone along have made it possible to achieve this brilliant success. In particular, Dr. Tarita achieved this success without any political or industrial background. During the last 25 years, Indira Group of Institutes have established various Institutions providing education in Primary and Secondary education, Management, Engineering, Information Technology, Arts, Science, Commerce, Pharmacy, Architecture and Design, etc. At present, the IGI group has blossomed to 12 Institutions delivering cutting edge learning to over 12000 students. In a sense, "from KG to PG", meaning Indira Group of Institutes, provides "Primary to Post Graduation education under one roof".

Dr. Tarita Shankar's brother, Professor Chetan Wakalkar has contributed greatly to this success of the Indira Group. Apart from this, Dr. Tarita emphasizes that the Board of Trustees of Indira Group, the Directors of the Institutes, Teachers and the non-teaching staff have contributed to this success. Although Dr. Tarita is satisfied with her journey today, she strives with her continual passion for innovation and always explores new avenues to ensure that her students always receive a high-quality education.

The students of the current generation face great problems not only in their academic life, but also in their personal life. Moreover, many students are exposed to various temptations, thus causing themselves harm. Such students need definite counselling. It was with this thought that she introduced the unique concept of "CARE CLUB". In this club, students and staff from Indira Group can meet Dr. Tarita to find ways to overcome the problems in their personal lives.

Talking about the initiative, Dr. Tarita says: "I started this initiative through social media to give personal advice to anyone in the Indira group. The Initiative which started on a small scale has grown so much that at least 10 students contact me through this program every week for personal advice. And the happiest part for me is that I can help the majority of them to find a solution to their problems."

Dr. Tarita's personal life has also been a guide to countless people. With great fortitude, she has overcome the constant ups and downs in her life and attained success. Her qualities are excellent oratory skills, ability to battle any problem courageously, and free, frank and fearless expression of her views. At the same time, her favourite passions are reading and travelling inquisitively around the world. It is because of this that she has visited most of the major countries around the world, and got acquainted and studied the culture and social life there. Above all, she loves to play her role as a mother of two loving sons. Dr. Tarita Shankar always insists that "Your work should reflect who you are." She has also received many awards recognizing her work.

Following are some of the major awards she has received in the last few years.

- Honorary Doctorate Degree in Management conferred by the Chitkara University, Chandigarh in the year 2011.

- Award for Distinguished Thought Leaders in the field of education by the World HRD Congress in the Year 2012
- Change Leader & Innovator Award by ET-Now
- Amongst Top 50 women in Education, Social Education and Entrepreneur Award at the World Education Congress 2017
- Education Entrepreneurship Award at the World Leadership Congress 2017
- Education Leadership Award, Women In Education Leadership Award (Excellence in Education) by ET Now Stars of The Industry in December 2018.

Keeping in mind that there is no age bar for learning new things, Dr. Tarita recently has completed the Owner-President Management Program [OPM] course from the prestigious Harvard Business School in the United States. Under the leadership of Dr. Tarita Shankar, the Indira Group celebrated its Silver Jubilee in the year 2019 and now they are exploring new horizons. There is no doubt that as in the last twenty-five years, Dr. Tarita Shankar will continue to be a source of inspiration and encouragement to many in the years to come.

Her Success Mantra:

'Successful leaders see the opportunities in every difficulty, rather than the difficulty in every opportunity'

About Dr. Ushy Mohan Das

Professor Dr. Ushy Mohan Das is a renowned doctor, a scientist researching linguistics and Communications, and founder president of Doctors against Corruption (DAC). An ardent academic, a behavioural psychology researcher, writer, globally esteemed keynote speaker, voice coach, multiple times TEDx speaker and a sought-after meditation, energy and leadership coach for more than three decades.

Numerous people have enjoyed the warmth, humour, and transformation power of her mind and self-development workshops. She is a globally esteemed mind and public speaking mastery coach, often referred to as Dr. Tongue Fu. A recognized authority on the psychology of leadership, negotiations and organisational turnaround, she is the creator of the widely-acclaimed brand "The Mind Workshop". She has conducted workshops globally for corporate houses, the government, faculty, students, sports professionals and bureaucrats.

She is the Founder CEO and Takumi at the acclaimed start up, Dr. Ushy's Wisdom Works. Dr. Das has now established a 360-degree energy wellness network called "Plus You Wellness," which organises monthly meet-ups in Bangalore, helping citizens become more mind aware and health conscious by offering simple solutions to deadly maladies.

MY STORY

Everything that I do I do for the truth

I did not become an entrepreneur by choice. Fifteen years ago, after working for 25 years as a doctor within a system that was rotting from within, I raised my voice against all the deep-rooted corruption I saw. As a result, I was not rewarded, instead threatened and sacked from a job that was dearer than life itself. At a crossroad, life offers choices. I was told to compromise and get back my job. I chose what my soul was committed to: to stay only with the truth.

Always remember that weak choices disempower and defeat you. To live defeated is to die every single day. I walked out of the highest chair in the campus to begin head butting the filthy corrupt systems established since years in medical education. A bitter yet empowering truth one needs to swallow every single day. "This is your life, own it," I told myself.

When patients place their life with a certain degree of trust in your hands it is as important for the doctor to receive them with dignity and treat with care.

I chose to be a doctor to nurture and add value to lives. I chose to be a healer to alleviate the pain of my patients. I encountered everything to the contrary. I started seeing myself as a warrior. There was no looking back ever since.

I took it upon myself to follow the burning purpose of cleansing a dark deep rooted gory system of medical and dental education. A life that has been dedicated to reforming and transforming what stands in the way of an honest, transparent fair system which treats people with the merit they deserve and not the merit they reserve. Thus, was born the selfless crusading team Doctors Against Corruption. There is no such thing as overnight success. My battles were not fought on my smartphone, but by looking in the mirror.

I got into the rotten system and knocked every door possible, starting from universities to the bureaucracy and ministry to throw light upon redundant archaic laws which needed to be abolished. In the beginning, I was ignored, and then laughed at, until the screams were so loud and the truth was so piercingly shrill that people in power were forced to listen. I fought legally too with my own personal investment and lo! and behold, became an 'overnight success' in ten years. I was ridiculed and ostracised by the community. I had every reason to give up groping in darkness. I could have grabbed the 'low hanging fruits' offered to me every single day, but I chose to fight on.

The first necessity was a single window entrance - the NEET. The first response was to shelve it. Change surely in a diverse country, dominantly rural and in lacking a common curriculum, is indeed a daunting task.

RTI after RTI was filed with its daily dose of bitter medicine called 'threats to life'. Guess, I needed to live to see the purpose being driven even more strongly. After filing writs and fighting for years now, NEET, which was deemed impossibility, came through. Resilience is what kept me at it until it was defrosted, and now is the hottest subject being discussed.

I knew I was a strongly persistent soul. I surely belonged to a group of people who saw their lives as having a higher purpose than simply earning a living. The redundant previous loophole-ridden acts needed to have been abolished and that was indeed a gargantuan task. No task is too big or small. It is surely how the mind sees it. All the corrupt were exposed, both individuals and institutions. I have been attacked enough on television debates for years as I was one amongst the few who took the side of the profession and the patient.

I kept pushing myself in spite of the inevitable obstacles that challenged me every day. After a decade, the National Medical Commission and National Dental Commission will see light of the day. We expect a lot from our society and systems. But that's not the way the world works. You don't control people. You only control yourself. It is still a long arduous task and I am hopeful. Disposal of flaws take time and requires humongous efforts by those not greedy for power.

Pain makes me more compassionate, more self-aware, more forgiving, and more tolerant. It hardens my core, yet softens my edges, which is the best way to live a healthy and balanced life. This crusade has enabled me to bear the brunt and wrath of many of the high and mighty. You must find the message behind your pain. You must clearly understand how this pain will help you get closer to the change you are seeking eventually. There is always a gap between who we are and how we reveal ourselves to the world. We have unexpressed dreams and truths which we often put in our shadow. There is a trick I learnt during this whole single-woman- standing army battle with the system - be courageously vulnerable and own those shadows before they own you. I never let the world dictate who I am or dilute my purpose.

I am a crusader against any kind of injustice I come across. Adding value to others' lives is a way of life for me. Today, thousands of patients and their kith and kin reach out from across the globe to seek solutions when they feel strongly let down by a system. Systems needed to be challenged and combated until they exist for the common good of the patient. Healthcare is not merely a business venture, as it seems to be the case today. It also needs to be a heartfelt, mindful service and only those cognizant of this must pursue medical education.

I am creating aware communities with monthly meet-ups called Plus You Wellness to help communities/citizens understand the concept of wellness more than illness as we live in a fast-paced success-driven society. We are human beings, not human doings.

I don't know what life ahead has in store for me. But I am sure that brave warriors like me will never rest in peace, even in death. We belong to a tribe who will rather die fighting on our feet than live begging on our knees. I am merely an artisan with a strong purpose in pursuit of truth. I refuse to be half-hearted in my efforts and am committed to a burning purpose all through my life. I am merely a humble takumi. To me, work is my own reward.

My mantra for success is: When your soul burns with purpose and passion, it's your duty to be burnt to ashes by it.

About Ms. Nabomita Mazumdar

Nabomita Mazumdar is a Mumbai based businesswoman. She has attained her MBA degree in HR from XLRI Jamshedpur. She is a Human Resources (HR) industry and thought leader in future of work. She is also into HR community lifecycle management, workplace design management. She blends relevant industry experience with new-age Internet startups in HR in India.

Nabomita has been awarded various honours such as '100 Women Achiever by Ministry of Women and Child Development', Felicitated during Rajmata Vijay Raje Scindia Birth Centenary celebrations at Talkatora Stadium in Delhi, Top 10 Inspiring Indian Entrepreneurs by Asia Tech Podcast, Top 10 Thought Leaders on Future of Work by Blue Jeans Network, Best 100 Young Speaker Award Cambridge English in Asia 2011 Western Region, Top 25 Influential Women on Twitter as per CIOL.com', Top 16 Entrepreneurs in India by Women of Jaipur, Ranked 2nd in Top 20 HR Influencer in Social Media by SHRM India 2015, ' Top 100 Tech Influencers', Top 15 Thought Leaders for Future of Work by Silicon India and many more'.

MY STORY

Why I became an entrepreneur

The joy of bringing people together for a cause is unparalleled. Creating value is what drives me. It started during the final term at XLRI Jamshedpur when a presentation was made on HR Communities. Nabomita felt that there could be more to it. When she met Dr. Madhukar Shukla, the Faculty for Building Learning Organisations, and discussed about it, he asked me to make an HR Community that would be omnipresent, free-to-use with great work-related discussions and every document related to work available for free.

I felt inspired and started looking for ways to form such a community. I eventually started an offline chapter that grew to many offline chapters across the country and even abroad. This started the journey of building communities.

I served as a Partner for the online community, serving nearly three million professionals solving business challenges for free, worldwide. I executed the growth strategy of the community successfully, leading the product to top-three in HR Communities in the world from 2010 to 2016 as per Alexa (while I was at the helm).

The community offers an online knowledge base and a discussion forum connecting the organisation's owners and its employees. Nearly 200,000 professionals visit the site daily to seek solutions related to their work. The community also offers a free-to-use database that includes information one might need at the office, right from manuals to forms to any document to refer for legal and official work.

There are no subscription or membership charges applicable for any of this support. It's entirely a 'free-to-use' community. It is one of the largest online HR communities in the world. The online site is involved with connecting people to solutions through live and virtual interactions, thereby impacting careers and companies, resulting in a positive revenue flow.

The mission of my business

Nabomita.com is a platform for evangelism, amplifying meaningful messages to society. We create communities for brands, corporates, startups and educational institutions. We evangelise cause, product and practice. We built the largest community for HR and thereafter many business communities, connecting millions of businesses worldwide, solution to their problems, impacting revenue in millions. We are a Media-tech firm with people working from different geographies.

We build communities both in online and offline formats. We have built niche, closed, gated and even forums privy to few. We have managed communities as large as a million members and even more. The footprint in community building and management has been 3 million, 22 million, 1 million, 4.5 million, and many smaller private communities. We evangelise cause, product, and practice for our client, where their target group of users or consumers turn into brand ambassadors for them.

We have enabled business, finance, retail, investor and healthcare companies to build and manage communities. This gets them client-ready markets. We work in both niche and mass markets as community building depends on the product the client sells. The numbers run in millions both in terms of reach and cost.

We help companies scale up their business and turn them around, earning million-dollar revenues. We mentor CEOs, CXOs and startup founders. We are on the board to eminent startup communities as an advisor and mentor. We have built technology products and communities that ranked first in the world. We work closely with organisations such as the United Nations and ICT promoting women's education in technology and management.

As a TEDx Speaker, I have been addressing forums across the world. I have been quoted in prominent national and International media, including

Forbes US. Nabomita.com is our platform to evangelise causes and issues such as Technology, AI, Future of Work, Investment, Startups, Employer Branding, Women Empowerment, Entrepreneurship, Gender Diversity and Equal Pay.

My failures and successes

I started my firm with zero capital building to what it is now. I have served the largest clients in the industry, bootstrapped and working lean. Each of my products is a pioneer in the market. We started building it when there was no demand for it. We created profitable firms.

When we started building the community, the word media-tech did not exist even in Silicon Valley.

When our product ranked highest on Alexa Internet ranking, ahead of US Gov. Website and Payscale Website, I was invited by Silicon Valley giants to brainstorm the disruption. Our journey was eventful, starting in India where the market was not even ready, to be celebrated by Silicon Valley. I am grateful to have received many awards for the work I have delivered so far.

What I learnt from my failures

We fail every day. Daily rejections and setbacks only push us to succeed. Failure is not the end result, it's a phase that prepares you for the better. Celebrate every fall and then pull yourself up to push ahead harder.

My advice to Startups

Start up only when you find your 2:00 am problem. Build only when you find that problem, that can keep you awake at 2:00 am. That one problem, which will push you beyond every limit and you will happily stretch. It will ask you for every sacrifice that you will proudly make, just to solve the problem.

My advice to women entrepreneurs

Women often are defined by limitations, be they mental, emotional, physical or societal. To every such limits and walls that stops women from growing, I wish to share that I built my first product from my living room with no investment. My second product started similarly. If I can do it, you too will. Find that problem that doesn't allow you to sleep at night and build a solution to it. The world is waiting to celebrate your hard work.

My Mantra for Success: The humility to fail takes the fear out of it.

MS. SHARMILA DIVATIA

MANAGING DIRECTOR
LAC VARDAAN ASSOCIATION, AN NPO

About Ms. Sharmila Divatia

I am a visiting faculty at Ali Yavar Jung National Institute of Speech & Hearing Disabilities, Bandra West, Mumbai. I have been lecturing on Accessibility and Universal Design for the Post Graduate (MA) course on Media and Disability Communication under the aegis of Mumbai University since 2012-13. I lead a California-based NPO Voice of Specially Abled Persons – VoSAP – Vadodara Chapter. I am a part of the Consortium for Inclusive Education in the city. Along with Bringle Academy, I have the NPO, Vardaan, for these activities.

MY STORY

I was born in New Delhi in September 1964 and spent my initial childhood years there, but was raised in Baroda, Gujarat from the age of five. My education and my spine of steel were groomed here in Gujarat. I am a disabled person. Having contracted and overcome encephalitis as a child, I have residual effects of the disease. I have a spastic left hand and a speech impairment – though these do not hinder me in my daily living.

With lots of patience and struggle I recovered my voice, eyesight, legs and part of my hand. I live, run marathons, swim, cycle and trek independently today. I am an entrepreneur and set up an NPO as well. I am busier than ever. I hold an MSc (Mathematics) degree along with a PG Diploma in Computer Science and an MBA (Operations). Professionally, I am a Six Sigma Black Belt and a software quality resource. I have been recognized for my work in the disability sector by NASEOH in December 2008 with an award.

My professional background of three decades in the IT industry – both in software delivery and business excellence practices has stood me in good stead. I have had a complete 360-degree view of varied businesses and practices. I started my career with the Indian dairy segment, moving to the country's financial institutions and various other sectors, like hospitality and travel, steel, mines, power, telecom, etc.

In my final assignment, at an MNC I was looking after shared services as well. In between learning business practices, I also learnt to put these efficiently via business transformation techniques and Six Sigma methodology. I am a resource for a lot of quality methods and practices – ISO, ITIL, CMMI, Six Sigma, etc. The brain needs challenges all the time and mine more so. Hence I switched from a software delivery director to a mere quality analyst at one point of time in my career. I also headed an MNC's IT Business Excellence unit. At this point, I was based in Mumbai.

By January 2015, I had completed my personal financial targets that I had set at the beginning of my career way back in 1989. I wished to go back home to Baroda, and take care of my ageing parents. I did move a year later, though I resigned from my job by April 2015. It took me a year to set up a base in my hometown and connect the dots all over again.

In early 2017, around January 26, I connected with an ex-colleague Anshav Jain, on a topic close to my heart, disability. Since I worked in the sector as a volunteer for sixteen years, he was checking if I could advise him on certain aspects of education with persons with disabilities. He had one such student in his academy. Our conversations became a regular feature over weeks and months. A lot of technology, disability, children and women-centric issues were discussed and debated. In September 2017, I signed on as a co-founder of Bringle Academy. I was an entrepreneur now, because I could not sit idly and let life pass by when I could do so much more with people who pulled at my mind-strings. I could not refuse challenges, since they built my strength and inner reserves every day.

Our vision at Bringle Academy is to make children future-ready and groom our young adults to take up productive work – be it a job or an entrepreneurial venture. We look to people to contribute in their own skill development as they grow in their careers.

My greatest failures were academic in nature. I am an encephalitis survivor and cerebral palsy is a side-effect of the disease I handle on a daily basis. My medication was Valium (a sleeping pill) throughout my academic career. I could never excel because medication and therapy prevailed over academics. My schooling was great, but throughout my college I suffered – both BSc. and MSc. were a terrible struggle with medication on.

My success came from both my academics and work - professional and volunteering. Post my college degree, I started to work and bloom in my career. I stopped medication and therapy. I took up a part time Diploma in Computer Science at the University and later an MBA (Operations) along with work.

Both academic certificates have an A+ and my career was much better with these two degrees. My best at work was the Quality Certification that I helped the company attain in 2010. In a similar vein, my Six Sigma Green/Black Belt course has an A+. A lot of my success is due to the fact that I do not know how to "Give Up". I was not taught this notion at home or in school. I give credit to my first boss, the late Mr. M L Shah, who taught a novice like me business and how to handle people.

While I bloomed late, a lot of other opportunities came my way in the form of volunteering in the disability sector. By the year 2000 I was well set in my career in Mumbai. My mother remarked once on one of my visits home that I should now look to help persons with disabilities as I had made a secure place for myself. I could help children, adults and ageing people too. It took me a few months to assemble the thoughts and act on it. I began as a judge on the Abilympics (National Abilympics Association of India) and went on to be a governing body member. I was a judge for regional, national and international events.

I had the honour to be a Member, Board of Directors of National Trust for the welfare of people with autism, cerebral palsy, mental retardation and multiple disabilities, Ministry of Social Justice and Empowerment, Government of India from April 2005 to March 2008. I then served as Member, Board of Directors of Association for Rehabilitation under National Trust Initiative of Marketing from April 2008 to March 2011.

I work with all governments when called upon to contribute on policy matters, be it the city, state or the country. I am associated with a number of NPOs across the globe to consult for and help people gain dignity and independent living. I swim, run marathons, trek and cycle. I love to read and listen to music, go to concerts and dance. I love riding motorcycles. I write articles when something touches my heart, and you will find my name in The Hindu in a few editions.

For me, failures are just aberrations. I do not consider my illness or my permanent disabilities as a failure of the medical team that worked on me fifty years ago. On the contrary, it is their perseverance that got me to walk, talk and see. My parents and school taught me to put negativity and people's attitudinal behaviour behind me and strive forward. A lot of the learning can be coalesced into one single thought – When patterns (traditional thought processes) are broken, new worlds emerge.

My advice to startups is you will encounter failure. Don't be disheartened. It is natural to be hurt when you fall down. Get up and start again. My father taught me this mantra, and I learnt it well.

My advice to women entrepreneurs is that gender bias is for people who are afraid to hand things over to women. So put the thought away that YOU can't do something big. Look at my founder and Investor – Anshav Jain – he has a majority of women heading his board and teams. I admire him because he really believes that women make better managers and leaders. He walks the talk. Few leaders in business do that.

My Mantra for Success is that I don't know how to string the words "give" and "up" together. So you will find me bouncing from a supposed failure right back on the winners table in a short span of time.

About Ms. Shabia Walia

Shabia Walia is a BSc in Chemistry and author of bestselling book Mamma Mania. Winner of the Rex Karmaveer Chakra Award for two consecutive years and also awarded with the TOP 50 Rising Stars Award by UK based We are the City, ICICI Advantage Woman Awards, Woman of Influence Award, WoW personality award, She The People Digital Achievers Award, Times She Unltd Award by Bombay Times and many more.

HER STORY

"The only regrets you have at the end of life are the chances you didn't take. So live your dreams and make them come true. Life's too short for procrastination."

Passionate, effervescent and forever in motion, Shabia is a whirlwind of energy and fun. After being a part of the entertainment industry for close to two decades, Shabia had begun to be disillusioned by the industry, the culture and its people. The erratic schedule coupled with her desire to spend quality time with her daughter had started to weigh on her mind. Lot of us have this habit of reading scraps of papers lying around, the stories behind classmate notes and the ingredients in the multitude of cosmetics we buy for us and our family. Shabia also had this habit, and every time she read the things that actually went into the soaps, creams, her concern grew. She was increasingly growing unhappy with the products she was using, especially for her daughter.

And one fine day on a cold January morning, a very simple recipe of a body scrub caught her attention. Armed with the knowledge that all the ingredients are available at her home, she set out to concoct it up. All done, and after bathing with it, she came out of the bathroom smiling. "I had an epiphany. That's how Wild Earth was born," grins Shabia. Wild Earth makes natural body products free of harmful chemicals. All their products are made with the best of natural ingredients and essential oils, and most importantly, handcrafted with love. The products range from soaps to luscious body butter to lip-smacking lip balms, sulphate free shampoos and delicious body scrubs.

A journey that began by using the products for self and close friends moved on to selling online for the first two years. We participated in exhibitions and the business started to grow by word of mouth. Being bootstrapped every leg of the way helped them to keep things under control and enhanced their growth. In its third year, the company scaled operations and now has got into retail in a big way. "Corporate gifting is another avenue where we do very well as our products make great gifts. We are also venturing into exports now," elaborates Shabia.

Being handmade and full of natural ingredients, Wild Earth has a huge target base. Anyone with a willingness to lead a healthy, natural lifestyle, be they women, babies, kids, men are their target audience. Wild Earth's products are safe for the entire family. Soaps, cream and scrubs that let us give our skin a royal treatment at affordable prices is their biggest selling point. Awesome quality and diligent customer service have let them enjoy great customer loyalty from the early stages.

A simple entrepreneur, Shabia strongly believes that if our intentions are right, the product is good, and you give its marketing the right spin, the venture is bound to make its mark. "Innovation is the name of the game and today the online space is a huge boon for new entrepreneurs like me. How you use it to your advantage is what sets you apart from the rest of them. Finally, there is no one in this world who will believe in your product more than you do. So make it the best, believe in it and then let your customers shout out loud for you. That's my mantra!"

A diligent student, hard-working daughter who never missed an opportunity to have fun, Shabia ensured that she never slacked in school and made good of the opportunities that came her way to earn and hone her skills. Working from the time of college instilled in her a great sense of handling money judiciously. "While my friends depended on their parents for pocket money, I ran my home. It was pretty empowering."

Today when her entrepreneurship has given her the boon of having a flexible schedule, Shabia's day starts off being a mom and rolls into the entrepreneur/boss mode after having a little me-time. She attends meetings, catches up with her people and sets out to conquer each day as her own. Being a hands-on entrepreneur, she does everything from packing, billing, the customer connects, etc. Evenings again are for friends and family. "The beauty of being an entrepreneur is being able to adjust your schedule as per your requirement," says Shabia.

Though the journey from corporate to entrepreneurship has had its own set of challenges, Shabia feels challenges only make it all exciting. "As an entrepreneur, your journey often gets lonely. Your wins and losses are your own. There is never a cut-off time. But taking them in your stride and remaining positive are keys to growth." Taking calculated risks, and an attitude that knows never to shy while seeking help have helped Shabia surmount the challenges that come her way.

"My friends and family are my biggest support. I never say no to an opportunity and never lose focus of why I became an entrepreneur. This pretty much takes care of most challenges. For the rest, I have an unbeatable positive spirit to take me through the worst." No wonder her husband calls her Luna – ek litre mein assi kilometer!!

An effervescent social person, Shabia tells us that social media, speaking platforms, and exhibitions are great ways to interact with people and make new clients. Good reviews of products and blogging are great tools to attract new customers too.

With a full-fledged support system in her family and friends and mentor, Shabia trudges on with their support in difficult times. "Lastly, my own positivity and never-say-die attitude keeps me from being depressed for more than a day. I am a fighter. I never accept defeat."

Today, Shabia manages two businesses with ease and elan. One is her media business where she writes and produces daily soaps and films and the second one being Wild Earth. "From daily soaps to bathing soaps" is how she describes her day. She also runs a Facebook group for Entrepreneurs called Idea To Income where she mentors new entrepreneurs through her own experiences. Recently she also launched a customised apparel and accessories brand called 'JunkFunk By Shabia'. She believes in creating multiple streams of income and also encourages others to do so.

Shabia herself is an inspiration to many. But who inspires her? "Stories of people who fought against the tide and became winners, givers who have assigned their lives for the betterment of the underprivileged, a good movie like Dangal or a book like Rich Dad, Poor Dad, all inspire me. My mother is my biggest inspiration. To have single-handedly brought us up without ever wallowing in self-pity was hugely inspiring. My daughter inspires me to be a good role model for her. I learn from everyone as I believe each one is unique and special."

Shabia's mantra for success: "I am the writer of my life film and I choose to be the hero rather than the victim. Life is too short to live by someone else's expectations of you!"

About Ms. Manisha Raisinghani

She was listed among the Top 25 Tech Trailblazers by Forbes. She has won awards, accolades and admirers alike with her technically astute but strategically exploratory mindset. Within a short period of time, she has led LogiNext to the level of global acceptability and recognition. She is actively involved in mentoring young entrepreneurs to enable them to realize their potential. Some of her mentees have gone on to become grand successes in their respective fields. With her experience of converting an idea into an exponentially growing enterprise with a multi-million-dollar turnover, year on year, she has become a sought-after advisor on the board of many different companies. She is also an influential mentor at Facebook's SheLeadsTech initiative.

MY STORY

I'm the Co-founder and CTO of LogiNext, the leading SaaS company, LogiNext is a transportation automation platform. Always passionate about technology, I decided to pursue my post-graduation from Carnegie Mellon University, which was a game-changing experience for me. With the much-coveted degree in Management Information Systems, I joined IBM as a partner.

From 2010 onwards, there was a huge inflow of technology trends like Machine Learning, Artificial Intelligence, Hyperautomation. Back then, these technologies were research buzzwords and not put in practical use. Alongside this, we also saw the parabolic smartphone penetration across the world. It was complemented by changing consumer trends who wanted access to everything at the touch of their smartphones.

Rather than physically visiting a store, getting items home-delivered became the rage. The customers drove exceeding expectations by wanting deliveries on the same day. Besides, digital maps as a category also evolved. People started accessing the map not just to find the route but also to understand the time taken to reach a particular destination. In today's day, even though we commute from home to work daily, there is a practice to check the ETA on the map for the known routes. Since people were indulging in this practice, it became more obvious that enterprises would definitely want to introduce this technology in tracking their parcels. Keeping this futuristic reality in mind, Dhruvil, my co-founder, and I decided to work on the transportation automation platform - LogiNext.

LogiNext ensures that your parcels reach you on time. Every minute 150,000 parcels are shipped worldwide. This is the tremendous size of the opportunity that the market holds. But how will one determine which parcel should be loaded in which truck and delivered in what sequence? Currently, the trends from price and features are shifting towards customer experience. With a number of options available, the customer is spoilt for choice and tends to purchase an item even if it is a little expensive as long as he can get it faster.

But determining the solution to this complex problem by manual means is error-ridden and estimating the accurate arrival times are next to impossible. There are so many factors involved in the delivery process, like traffic conditions, weather, priority customers, order spoilage, preferred delivery window, size of the parcel that a robust technology is needed to consume these data points to give an exact time of arrival.

To deal with this complex scenario, artificial intelligence and machine learning come into play. In the last three years, LogiNext has processed over one billion parcels and the software just gets smarter with each parcel we process on the system as it learns from the user behaviour and optimises the following time when an order is placed. Now more than 150 enterprise companies lean on LogiNext.

Logistics is a traditional industry and amongst the last ones to place a foot in the door for technology and innovations. There has to be a culture shift to accommodate change and the logistics industry counterparts have lagged behind in this. To bring about this substance-change in the industry was long pending. We touched the core of the business and built our product with umpteen empathy and also sold it to them in their own voice. That's when we saw usage, acceptance and finally the epiphany of the solution's vitality.

Building the LogiNext business has been super interesting and we have consistently optimised our operations to perfection. For instance, when we started out, to test our product and get feedback, we sold to small and medium enterprises. The sales effort was demanding and the sales cycle was long, the return on investment was low. Considering this, we took a paradigm shift in our strategy and decided to focus on pure-play enterprise companies. To get an initial breakthrough was difficult in the enterprise companies, but in the long run, it turned out to be a better bet. Now, we are proud to be easing and optimising the logistics process for over 10 Fortune 50 customers.

Success did not come knocking on the door - there were sleepless nights, fast turn-around for customers, volumes of SOWs to be read and implemented, challenging deployments - but these are the things I dig. It was exciting for me. It is what keeps me up at night - thinking and dreaming about what can we do to thrill our customers. What I love about LogiNext is the great team that is super customer focused and just gets things done.

One of the defining moments for us was when we cracked an arduous implementation in Lithuania. We had to work alongside them despite the language barrier and contrasting time zones. The implementation was with a company that was using archaic technology infrastructure and did not have much experience in dealing with modern systems. But our team was able to make both ends meet in a stipulated period of time, bringing about a seamless integration with their systems and now they are one of our biggest customers in Europe. To date, this remains really close to my heart, as it reminds me to never give up even in the most difficult situation.

Good things don't come easy. So if you want good things, you have to enjoy the rocky path to reach there. It's great to be successful in the first go, but success doesn't teach you as much as failure does. Failure is the inception of learning something new and we should embrace both failure and success equally.

In fact, the success mantra for startups is to get comfortable with the unknown and have a risk-taking appetite. Be persistent, but know when to let go. When starting out, do everything and anything, never undermine the power of a phone call or a coffee meeting. It might be intimidating to see so many of the peers making noise, but stay focused on your plan, work hard every single day to reach your goal.

But like any new journey, this ride hasn't been hunky-dory. Being a woman entrepreneur in the logistics industry was a brow-raiser. Every time Dhruvil and I would be at a conference, the delegates would be surprised to know that I am running the technology and Dhruvil the business - such was the attitude towards women in the industry.

Given the opportunities available around us, the best time to pursue dreams is now, and one must not let go of them without giving them a chance. I especially believe that this is the time for women to march alongside men and follow their aspirations. Working with so many prolific women, I strongly regard that, notwithstanding the gender, you can achieve whatever you set your heart to. At this time and age, women should not be fighting for equal rights, but should be fixating on their ambition.

Women have stepped into traditional industries and disrupted them with innovations - whether it is logistics, banking, education, legal or government. They have stirred the modern industries and have become the prime faces in domains like Aeronautics, Design, Virtual Reality, Automation. I am proud to be a woman who makes an impact. I encourage all women to venture out, start up or work for the cause that you believe in. I stand by this - that a gender barrier does exist - it is a glass ceiling above your head - but only till you don't step up and break it. The barrier is in your mind. Get past it and it will open doors to a world of opportunities and possibilities. Go out and grab what is yours.

My Mantra for Success: Think Big - Achieve your next 3 years plan in the next 12 months.

MS. JAYA VAIDHYANATHAN

CHIEF EXECUTIVE OFFICER
BCT DIGITAL (A BAHWAN CYBERTEK GROUP)

About Ms. Jaya Vaidhyanathan

She is the CEO of BCT Digital, a global technology company specialising in Digital Transformation, Predictive Analytics and IoT. She holds a computer science and engineering degree from Madras University, a management degree from Cornell University, and also earned a CFA charter. In the last twenty-five years, she has managed multi-billion portfolios in large multinationals. Her career began as an investment banker with Wall Street firms, and journeyed through organisations such as HCL, Accenture and Standard Chartered Bank (Scope). She is a three-time winner of the prestigious Stevie Award, including a Lifetime Achievement Award for Women in Business in 2019. She also received the 'Business Leader of the Year' from Asian Business Leadership Forum and the 'Innovator of the Decade' from IWLF. She is a member of the New York Security Analysts Society and serves on several international boards such as Altran Technologies and UTI AMC. She also serves on the board of an NGO, Mastermind Foundation.

MY STORY

I began as an investment banker with Wall Street firms and have worked at the intersection of the technology and financial services spectrum. I have been responsible for the business transformations of several Fortune 100 clients, managing large teams, and transforming greenfield businesses into large corporates. As the CEO of BCT Digital, I manage end-to-end business operations, expansion plans, P&L, and go-to-market strategy. As an 'intrapreneur at BCT Digital, I am responsible for product innovation and ensuring market success.

Such exposures and successful implementations were possible with a focused vision in my mind. My vision is to make the Indian market stronger. Hence, after having worked with Wall Street, I felt the need to bring value-based IT jobs to India. I then joined HCL and facilitated outsourcing multi-million worth deals, creating thousands of job opportunities for engineers in India. I then moved to Accenture, managing their large deals portfolio. This focus continued in my latter roles as well – as an Executive Vice President of Standard Chartered Bank (Scope), heading strategic transformation and technology. In 2014, I joined as an 'intrapreneur' at BCT Digital and kick-started the FinTech initiatives to drive digital transformation for banks and financial institutions through our risk management product suite rt360, and focus on building India as a product innovation hub.

Along with product innovation, we want to ensure market success through the trend of 'Reverse-Innovation' – build world class products for the Indian banking system to address its complex issues, like rising NPAs, financial inclusion, liquidity crisis, etc - and further innovate the Global FinTech space. We leverage disruptive technologies, such as AI, predictive analytics, Big Data to solve a yet-unsolved business problem and continue to adopt technologies as they emerge.

We are focused on the credit and operational risk areas and have many niche products. One such product, the Early Warning System (EWS), identifies stressed accounts early on and improves NPA recovery and profitability.

Traversing through these milestones wasn't easy. Successes and failures together helped destine the journey. One of my biggest failures was when I was working with a tech major. A critical deal fell through just days away from closure. Despite all the hard work we had put in as a team, this set us back by a whole year simply due to an untimely acquisition that got in the way. For both me and the team, it was certainly the lowest point in our careers. However, that turned out to be my greatest high as well.

Just a year later, we were back in the game. The same deal went through, and it was twice as big as what it was to start with. For me, the biggest takeaway was the social impact – the deal created jobs for over 6,000 engineers in India. At a particularly tough time (Y2K), it was a silver lining.

The next best success is the launch of the NPA product that has a huge impact in putting back millions of dollars per bank per year through Early Warning Systems.

From such experiences, I learnt that, the lowest lows are bound to become integral parts of our career success. It is important to consider failures as valuable learning experiences. If you don't fail, it means you have not really set the bar high enough.

Such an attitude is essential for those with new innovative minds entering the industry as we are seeing a rise in the number of start-ups. While the benefits of owning a start-up are obvious, being your own boss, developing from ground zero and of course reaping the fruits of the efforts, it is also critical to have a never-give-up attitude.

According to Harvard Business Review, 75 percent of start-ups dissolve in this journey. Hence never stop professionally building networks with the right people and at the right time. Be willing to take risks and start anew. Hire mentors with a lot of professional expertise.

My advice to all women entrepreneurs is to first accept that it is often hard to stay the course by balancing priorities in our lives. When the going gets tough, just remember that there are others before you that have paved the path. Dream big, stay focused on your priorities, network and Just Go Win. Most importantly, do take time off to focus on you – for a healthy body and mind are critical.

My Mantra For Success: If you never failed, it means you did not set the bar high enough. Dream big enough so that you fail, and have the courage to aim higher next time.

About Ms. Reema Sanghavi

Reema Sanghavi is the founder and Managing Director of Maximus MICE & Media Solutions, a decade old global, award-winning brand with a network of over 500 corporate clients spread across every continent and a repertoire of over 1,000 events. As a step towards women empowerment, she co-founded Pinkathon, which is now Asia's Largest Run for Women featuring over 1,00,000 women runners every year. She is also Director with the international speaker management agency, Speaking Minds, that is determined to redefine the B2B marketing scenario in India.

Reema Sanghavi has also been elected as the Vice President for the Event and Experiential Marketing Association (EEMA), the leading platform for information, education, networking and commercial opportunities, as well as the leading voice in government and the community for firms within the event industry. Over the years, Reema has been conferred with several awards, including MICE Future Leader of the Year Award, Femina Women Leadership Award, and many more for her contributions to business and industry.

She has always strived to raise the bar higher with each step, leaving a distinct trail of impactful experiences that have contributed significantly to the world of experiential marketing.

HER STORY

When Reema Sanghvi was born in Oman - the third daughter, a family eagerly hoping for a male child - her father was so upset that he didn't even bother to see her at the hospital. It was a national holiday. His dream of raising the next Sachin Tendulkar was shattered, and relatives weren't holding back from passing misogynistic taunts. Soon though, Reema became the apple of his eye, leaving no stone unturned to live up to all of his expectations. She excelled in sports, aced every math test. She even chopped her hair so short that the local barber mistook her for a boy.

Reema's father passed away due to a heart attack when he was just 46 years old. The business empire he built instantly collapsed, leaving Reema, her sisters and mother vulnerable and grief-stricken. Reema was sent to her maternal aunt's home in Kolkata, so that she could pursue the rest of her studies. Reema's transition from Oman to Kolkata set the foundation for an important cornerstone of resilience - knowing how to navigate adverse circumstances, adapt smoothly, transition quickly and make the very best of life's lemons.

Reema's destiny eventually took her to Mumbai. When working at a call centre, she realised her true passion - organising events that would inspire others. So, she took the initiative to head the events committee at her workplace, creating a new role for herself within the company, rather than staying in a rut. Eager to explore her passion further, Reema joined Platinum Events, where she understood the importance of being able to implement her own ideas in her own way.

In 2008, when she lost a huge portion of her savings in the stock market crash, rather than feeling bogged down, she looked at it as an opportunity to no longer have any inhibitions. There was no longer anything else to lose, and so following in the footsteps of her parents, who were both successful entrepreneurs, Reema took the plunge and pursued her dream of forming her own events company - Maximus MICE Media Solutions Pvt Ltd.

The journey ahead wasn't a bed of roses though. Within nine short months, one of her two business partners jumped ship. Rather than giving up, Reema took this as an important lesson in learning how to rise above and beyond your challenges, assess potential risks rather than taking things at face value blindly. She forged ahead with more determination and built an empire that has stood the test of time for over a decade.

Today, Maximus MICE Media Solutions Pvt Ltd holds a coveted position as one of the top 25 event companies of India, with many awards to tout, and a vast network of over 500 corporate clients spread across continents. Her most celebrated brainchild - Pinkathon - Asia's largest run for women - has been transforming the lives of thousands of women as they run freely towards a healthier and empowering lifestyle, one marathon at a time. Pinkathon is no more an event, it's a revolution.

She incepted Speaking Minds, a B2B knowledge solutions company, and also runs an NGO called United Sisters Foundation. She is also Vice President - West for the Events and Entertainment Management Association, serving the events industry at large. Through this professional journey, Reema went through two miscarriages and the demise of the most important person in her life, her mother Kalpana. Reema and her sisters adopted an elephant in her memory and called her Kalpana. She believes that if there is any deed she is proud of in her life, it's this adoption.

Reema's work has earned her many accolades, including the MICE Future Leader of the Year Award, Femina Women Leadership Award, 50 most powerful women in the world of MICE, and many more…

Reema's Mantra for Success: Live to Inspire.

MS. TANUL MISHRA

FOUNDER & CEO
AFTHONIA PVT. LTD

About Ms. Tanul Mishra

I have been making a mark as the founder of India's foremost FinTech incubator and FinTech startup mentor. We all must have come across the famous African proverb that says, "If you want to go fast, go alone. If you want to go far, go together." This perfectly defines my entrepreneurial journey. I have constantly believed that working in a collaborative manner acts as the best tool for achieving success.

When I started building Afthonia, the one thing that I was certain about was that it will not be a one-person endeavour. Afthonia is a combined function of our team, most importantly, the panel of advisors and mentors that have come on board.

My journey before Afthonia over the two decades of my career span, I have worked in diverse domains, including media, telecom and also in the early dotcom industry. I moved on to INOX as the Alliance Manager, where I was involved in creating long term strategic tie-ups and exploring avenues to maximize direct revenue. As Manager - Alliances at Tata Communications/VSNL, I contributed towards retaining and attracting Broadband (BB) subscribers by providing Value Added Services on the VSNL Broadband network. I also worked at striking partnership deals with content aggregators.

MY STORY

In 2009, when I joined PayMate, a tech-led B2B payments firm, adoption of digital finance was still at a budding stage. The FinTech story was cautiously unfolding. Startups were intensively creating new business models. Payment solutions, bill payments and recharge areas were the centre of attention. During my stint in the FinTech space at PayMate, I contributed towards building the company's core B2B segment and conceptualizing long-term revenue streams. My key contribution was towards setting up a payment model that is delivering exceptional results for the organization till date. During my tenure with PayMate, the revenue grew exponentially and resulted in functional expansion of the B2B business for the company.

These were early days for the payment industry and it gave me a first-hand insight on emerging financial technologies and their impact on the changing landscape of the economy. It allowed me to get clarity on tech innovations and their contributions to address market challenges. Any FinTech company has the potential to build scale out of untapped opportunities in the country, but it means addressing challenges that come from India being a diverse and multicultural country with low awareness of FinTech services.

Working with a startup surged my entrepreneurial aspirations. Soon after my tenure with PayMate, I ventured towards my own entrepreneurial journey with Shipra Bhansali, my Co-founder, as we built Eatelish. Eatelish is a food service bringing artisan food makers across India directly to the doors of consumers. During our journey, the team has established a robust supply chain that enables sourcing of local food, organization of recipes, alignment of ingredients and doorstep delivery. Today, Eatelish has over 25 suppliers with a presence in 21 stores across India. We exited after seven years, early in 2019.

As we were building Eatelish, there were many highs and lows. The one thing that we missed having was a support system. We missed having an environment that was safe to test in and one that would open doors for us. My entrepreneurial journey gave me visibility into the challenge areas and also the constant state of flux of an ever-evolving landscape. Having a strong background in FinTech had prepared me for the road ahead and had given me an understanding of the space.

The beginning of an entrepreneurial sojourn in FinTech

When it was time to ask myself what I wanted to do next, I realized that I was keen to work with early-stage startups. My intention was to help them create and build the product, establish company culture and raise funding by establishing a support network that the startups could leverage. That's how Afthonia Lab came into being. An incubator focused on FinTech, Afthonia is unique in its vision of sharing world class knowledge from mentors across developed markets such as the US and Europe.

The approach is simple - to ensure that FinTech startups have the highest opportunity of success by gathering knowledge from across the world, understanding best practices for a market like India and customising these insights to fit the company. We follow an approach that is different from a classroom or cohort approach. We follow a well-analysed selection procedure for the startups that we incubate. We go through an in-depth study of the challenges or stage of growth. Each of our startups is inducted with single or multiple mentors depending on the domains that need to be worked upon. This ensures securing structured learning programs and key market connections.

We have successfully intubated a startup that was at an idea stage and have got it funded. Another startup that we worked with was at prototype and now has launched its service. For one of the startups, we collaborated with a global investment advisor who worked with the company on streamlining the product. Also, we had an UI/UX mentor who contributed towards fine-tuning the company's operations. Now they have access to customers internationally under the guidance of a global mentor.

We had another startup which was at the idea stage. So, firstly, we aligned them with an advisor who assisted them on product development and building a business model. We worked vigorously with them on business structuring and capital management.

It has been a very fulfilling journey so far. In the past few months, we have worked with and seen early-stage startups grow from scratch. There is still a lot to be learnt and questioned through the challenges and experiences as we scale ahead.

Challenges and successes along the way

An entrepreneur's journey is always challenging. It's like running an obstacle race. I started working when I was 21 years old, and ever since I have been financially self-dependent. So when I decided to bootstrap with Eatelish, I was reinvesting everything I had back into the business, not knowing if and when it would pay off. I also knew that as a woman it would be difficult to go back to a career after an entrepreneurial break.

When we were setting up 'Eatelish', we had to make choices between multiple critical requirements. Since the company was essentially product oriented and a bootstrapped unit, many a times it was a challenge to keep things on the good side of the sail. Further, when I founded Eatelish there's a very interesting question that we were asked frequently: "Is this a hobby project?" This made the journey more difficult, because as an entrepreneur when we're talking about our business, instead of focusing on the virtue of the business or the problem that we're solving, we had to actually take a step back, prove our intent to run the business and our ability to sustain it as a bootstrapped unit.

The rewarding experience of building Eatelish and exiting it at a valuable stage is one of my key milestones in life. When somebody buys your business, it's a validation that what you've created and set up is of significance and merit. Another important milestone is the inception of Afthonia Lab as a FinTech incubator. It was a unique operation model that had not yet been explored in India. Since it was a less treaded path, it demanded large volumes of insight, research and risk appetite.

Through all the challenges, I've learnt to be flexible towards changing business environments. Running a startup is a progressive discovery. One is not going to achieve hockey stick growth and overnight successes. It is important to always evaluate one's journey to date and recalibrate when needed.

If being an entrepreneur is tough, being a businesswoman is double the challenge. Subconscious gender biases, low confidence stemming from societal stereotypes, child care and family responsibilities, lack of access to finance, and safety issues are just a few concerns to name. But a woman's entrepreneurial journey can kick start and go a long way only when she herself makes a decision to support it. There are of course abundant challenges she has to battle and could do with some support.

The past decade closed with 20 percent of startups worldwide raising their first funding round in 2019 having a female founder (source: https://tinyurl.com/yv4a7khz). In India, the landscape of women entrepreneurship still has a long way to go. Half of the Indian population is female. The value that women entrepreneurs can bring to the table is unprecedented in terms of employment creation, innovation, driving social change by encouraging fellow women entrepreneurs and economic growth. A recent study predicted that in India, strategic measures to close the gender gap could lead to a 6.8 percent gain in GDP (source: Purva Khera, "Closing Gender Gaps in India: Does Increasing Womens' Access to Finance Help? "IMF Working Paper No. 18/212, September 2018).

My advice to women professionals has always been that, when you walk into a room, whether you're running a business or you're a working professional, walk in without a gender. If there's a bias, that's the other person's problem and not yours. As an individual yourself, be sure never to let gender interfere with your work performance.

Mantra for Success:

My leadership mantra is to trust my team wholeheartedly. I strongly believe in empowering my team and enabling them to become leaders themselves. One doesn't need to be a founder or a CEO to be a leader.

If you look at a business, there are many roles: customer service, business, human resources, etc. Culture is a thriving, living entity and it is essential to have really good leaders in every team and at every stage of the business to keep the culture alive. Each stage of life and also every phase of the business gives one an opportunity to step into a leader's shoes and make a difference that will create a positive impact in the space around them - with their clients, teams and ultimately the organization. I constantly endeavour to create more leaders in the company, because they will then be able to take the vision of the company ahead as it scales.

One must also focus on the big picture at all times. Keep the focus ahead, learn from one's mistakes and gain from challenges. I think Rumi expresses it perfectly when he says "Try not to resist the changes that come your way. Instead let life live through you. And do not worry that your life is turning upside down. How do you know that the side you are used to is better than the one to come?"

MS. NEHA KANABAR

FOUNDER
COMMUNITY ENTREPRENEUR
UNIMO UNIVERSE OF MOMS

About Ms. Neha Kanabar

A National Training Head by profession, a radio jockey by passion and the Founder of UNIMO Universe Of Moms, arguably the world's largest community of mothers with 3.45 lakh digitally connected moms on Facebook & Whatsapp.

UNIMO has a presence in 21 chapters globally to drive more local & geo tagged connect for mothers.

She was a Global Lead for "Facebook Community Leadership Circles" - Mumbai. Professionally, Neha is a corporate trainer specialising in the domain of Digital Marketing & Sales for the last sixteen years & an EQi2.0 certified professional who has worked for renowned organisations like Times of India, Unilever, IFB & ABD. Neha is an engineer & an MBA with specialisations in Marketing and HR.

She is a member of the Power Admins group of Facebook. She is the mother of twin boys. Her philanthropic work is primarily around her own vertical - UFF Unimo Freedom Fighter, through which she drives change at the ground level, UFF adopts orphanages, senior citizen homes, conducts drives around pertinent social causes. It is also associated with renowned NGOs like Goonj. Neha is a renowned mommy influencer and her story has been covered by multiple media platforms. Neha is also a certified Manifestation Coach.

MY STORY

Why I became an entrepreneur

I am not just an entrepreneur, but also a community builder. Communities can start revolutions. Communities can bring change and be powerful and humble at the same time. No other business could have given me this kind of USP. So I chose to become one saw that there was a dire need of hyperlocal communities of mothers. So I created one.

Mission of my business

The mission of my community is to make the world a smaller and more connected place.

Successes and Failures

My successes are equivalent to the success of my community members.

During the lockdown, a mother died while delivering her baby and one of our moms enquired for breast milk on the community for this child. In spite of this critical period, two lactating moms came forward. While one expressed her willingness to give milk, the other mother visited the nursing home and fed the baby. Aren't these beautiful stories of humanity? This whole act of support and humanity was also published by Fox News.

My community also supports small mompreneurs to sell on our platform free of cost. It also helps them connect with the right mentors and experts through our multiple workshops and events.

My failures aren't my failures, but a limitation which I strive to overcome. We want to grow our community and start making more impact in the space of domestic violence.

My advice to startups

Create a unique solution, don't just blindly copy. It is good to be inspired, but copying something will not take you far. Whatever is your passion, pursue it. Don't think and analyse it for a long period.

Belief, execution and action matter more than sheer planning.

My advice to women entrepreneurs

We women are engineered very beautifully, but if we don't stretch, we rust. Don't rust fellas!

My Mantra for Success: If beautiful things happen inside you, beautiful things will happen outside you.

MS. SHIKHA PANDEY

ENTREPRENEUR, YOGINI & PODCASTER
BECK TECHNOLOGY VENTURES
PVT. LTD & PURNAYOG.COM

About Ms. Shikha Pandey

Always been entrepreneurial whether in my corporate stints or while building my own ventures. 7 years of building brands like HUL & Airtel and 9 years of building my own ventures – Gemini New Media Ventures LLP & BECK Technology Ventures Pvt. Ltd. Work experience spanning across marketing, lead generation, customer service, product UI design and flow, go to market strategy and implementation and brand building and recall. FMCG, logistics, travel, beauty and telecom are few of the sectors that I have been associated with.

MY STORY

Mine is the story of a converted entrepreneur.

Most people become an entrepreneur either because they hated their jobs and the routine that comes with it or they simply always knew that they were born to be entrepreneurs. Neither holds true for me. So here is my journey and my reasons to become an entrepreneur.

I graduated from SNDT Women's University, Juhu, in Mass Communication and in my third year took up an internship with a small size public relations (PR) agency where the founders threw me in deep waters almost immediately by giving me my own clients to handle. From there I moved on to Blue Lotus Communications Pvt Ltd, a PR & Ad Agency and worked on some interesting clients like J&J, Hellen Keller Institute, etc.

While handling PR for Carwale, Sherpalo Ventures & TiE Mumbai chapter, I found the whole startup and funding ecosystem very interesting. But never once did I imagine that I would be right in the middle of it all. While I loved doing what I was doing, my immediate goal was to move to the other side, handling larger roles in marketing. Soon enough, I got to be a part of the marketing team at Hindustan Unilever Limited (HUL) to launch Pond's Age Miracle in India. From there I moved on to being a part of the Brand & Marketing team at Bharti Airtel Limited.

I met my partner when at Airtel and we got thinking on building something together. Thus came the idea of Gemideals.com, my first venture, - a real estate bulk buying portal in Mumbai. We worked with real estate developers to list their under-construction property and create a group of buyers to buy multiple units at investor rates. The venture did take off and we cracked multiple deals, but eventually, the unorganized market and the slack in real estate led us to shut down the business.

For me, my interest was seeded in the entrepreneurial ecosystem during my first job and for my partner it was because of the various companies he had set up in his corporate avatar. We wanted to contribute to the growing startup wave in

India in our own way and thus was born my venture Gemini New Media Ventures (GNMV) Spaces - a co-working space born out of sheer love for startups.

We set up and launched the co-working space in 2014, when co-working as a concept was in its nascent stages in India. It was a time when we had to demystify the concept of people sharing their office space and the benefits of co-working. The space started with 40 seats and today we have over 200 seats running at 90 percent occupancy on an average. The addiction to building something of your own and bringing something new to the world to change the way things work is unmatched.

With GNMV Spaces attaining auto mode, my mind wandered off and started to think of something new to build. That is when the idea of BECKME was conceptualized as a same-day delivery service in Mumbai which later pivoted to BECKFriends.com - a traveller-powered delivery marketplace for travellers to monetize their unused luggage space by carrying verified packages on their travel routes. We are impacting the two largest sectors – Travel and Logistics by creating a segment where travel meets logistics. International shipping is a complex, expensive and time-consuming process for individuals looking to buy things from international markets or for SMEs looking to test out their products in global markets. BECKFriends.com simplifies the process of international shipping by enabling shipping through travellers.

The network enables travellers to sign up and post their travel plans, post verification and volunteer to carry packages on the marketplace for a price. The individual buyers and the SME shippers on the other hand sign up and share details of their shipping requests post verification. The matchmaking happens and the travellers get to earn as they travel and the shippers/buyers are able to ship anything anywhere in an economical and flexible manner. The network of verified travellers and buyers is further fuelled by 250+ travel agents and 400+ merchants empanelled as channel partners on a revenue-share model and can be accessed on the web or through a mobile app. The current traction is from India, USA, UK, Singapore, Hong Kong & Canada. It has not always been smooth sailing. While success is what everyone talks about, failures are what make us better.

So, two such learning experiences for me were when I started Gemideals.com, a bulk-buying real estate website. The business did generate revenues and I covered whatever I had invested, but it did not take off to the next level due to the unorganized real estate market and the overall slack.

This taught me that the sector and industry in which you operate is as important as your business idea. The scale, pace and returns on your business are dependent on the overall state of the industry too. The second one was to not let go off Gemideals sooner. Any startup is built with sweat, passion, and grit, and my venture was no exception. But still, it took me more than six months to agree and acknowledge that it was time to close this down and for the better.

I learnt to understand the signs my venture and the outside factors give me and the significance of timely closure and moving on. Now when I look back, the growth of GNMV Spaces as amongst the very few co-working spaces that are generating profits is my success story of how perseverance is as important as passion. We started before the dawn of the co-working era and moved into it with the early mover advantage proving that you have to keep building and be ready when it is time to reap the benefits of what you have sown. Another such decision that I would count as a success story worth sharing would be pivoting to become BECKFriends.com - a global delivery solution from BECKME.

It was at the onset of the Covid 19 Pandemic in June 2020 that I finally launched my dream project - PurnaYog, that enables people to live a more holistic life by drawing from the age-old wisdom of Yoga & Ayurveda. Through the PurnaYog platform, people of all age groups, across the world, have access to holistic living practices, right at their homes. The platform offers online sessions, one-on-one consulting, podcasts, wisdom talks, mindfulness & meditation practices, breath work and a great sense of community. And this venture, like my previous ones, is a reflection of my belief that a true entrepreneur is one that creates value & simplifies things.

Summarising all the entrepreneurial experiences of a decade, my advice to upcoming entrepreneurs would be that don't get into entrepreneurship because you think it is cool to be an entrepreneur. It is a lot of hard work, criticism, negativity and responsibility, fuelled by an unbelievable amount of conviction which will seem wearing out on most days. Become an entrepreneur because you know you can create an impact that will better the world or the lives of people in some way. Find the reason why you want to become an entrepreneur. Wanting to be an entrepreneur because it is cool or you have a terrible boss is not a good enough reason, as you will need much more than that to be an actual entrepreneur, leave alone to be a successful one.

To all the women entrepreneurs out there, let's just try not to label ourselves as some stereotypes in our own minds. Let's not have our gender define how good or bad we are at what we do. Also, let's not try too hard to prove ourselves and in the process take up the entire onus on ourselves.

No one is perfect and hence we too, like male entrepreneurs, need a team and co-founders. Let's delegate more and let our teams fill in for what we lack. Let's focus on building our strengths and improving on the things we lack. The journey of an entrepreneur is tough and lonely, so let's not make it worse by not reaching out for help just to prove that we are not less than anyone. Everyone needs help every now and then and a true entrepreneur is one who asks for it and makes the most of it (Holds true irrespective of gender).

My Mantra for Success: Don't be limited. Be a LIMITED Edition!

About Ms. Shridaa Raheja

An ardent professional, holding an experience of over 20 years plus in the field of Interior Design. Has hands-on experience of site project management. A Diploma holder, with enriched experience.

MY STORY

What would a girl from a humble family be ambitious about? I was the third daughter to my parents, who could barely cope with the expenses for this little girl called Anmol. Of course, now I am called Shridaa. I lived a simple life, but with a burning desire that I would never depend on anyone.

Life moved on. I got married, but both survival and education were difficult. I took some suggestions from well-wishers and joined a diploma course in interior design. I excelled in my studies and interned with my principal, who gave me the knowledge of all nitty-gritties faced on the site.

The only reason I became an entrepreneur was to be my own boss. Interior Design became my passion. Decoration was what I dreamt of. Initially, I wasn't even sure if I would be doing this in future or just passing it off as a subject learnt. But when I completed my internship and established my own office at the age of 22, in 1997/98, I realized that I had to make it. My motto then turned out to be - "The harder the situation, the bolder the stand I must take."

My failures and success stories

1. Asking my spouse to join me in my company.
2. Trusting friends and working on their projects at a low cost.

A lot of success did happen and roaring ones too. The two I want to highlight are:

1. Being an absolute fresher and when no one would entrust you with a big project, I decided to take up restoring an old bungalow into something magnanimous. I told the client not to pay my fee till he was completely satisfied. By the end of the project, the client and his family were so happy that besides paying me the fee, they couldn't stop appreciating and thanking me for the marvellous job.
2. Small stories - Working on contemporary interior design concepts in an era where traditional concepts were known and accepted. Worked as a faculty in a well-known university and gained supreme knowledge. I learnt about how commercial spaces can be used in an optimum way. Also learnt space management, budget management, working on timelines and much more...

My advice to startups

- Set a goal
- Make a Plan
- Stay focused
- Work Hard
- Succeed, and stay humble

Women Entrepreneurs, you are the future. Strike an idea and work on it. You can do it as you have it in you. You'll be praiseworthy if you resolve to work hard.

My Mantra for Success: No one can give you your goals. No one can dig for you. This is your journey.

About Ms. Namrata Tatiya

Namrata is an experienced Company Secretary and Advocate. She is the founder of Acculegal- Central India's fastest growing Startup centric- Legal financial company from Raipur Chhattisgarh. She is also the Promoter of Ashi Welfare Foundation. Recognized as one of the most impactful young women, she has been featured by various magazines and newspapers.

HER STORY

Namrata Tatiya is a source of motivation to all the young girls and youth in the state. Since school days, she has had the zeal to achieve big. Academics helped her get more clarity to choose the path to achieve the vision. Namrata is an experienced Company Secretary, an Advocate and a commerce graduate.

Namrata is a promoter of two entities today. She has founded Acculegal Services Pvt Ltd in 2017 and Asha Devi Foundation in 2019. Acculegal is Central India's fastest growing Startup-centric legal financial company from Raipur, Chhattisgarh.

In the past two years, Acculegal has crossed 250+ clients Pan India and is growing rapidly. With a demonstrated history of working in the corporate legal services industry, her interest also lies in Intellectual Property Rights and Education & Awareness.

With a mission to create awareness amongst startups, currently she is working on collaborations with universities and institutions in India. She is an impactful speaker and has conducted many sessions across India. Namrata is also an active volunteer at Headstart and is a mentor at many colleges.

Namrata hails from a religious Jain-Marwadi family. Coming from a tier three city where women never stepped out to do business, she has had a roller coaster journey so far.

Being the eldest in her generation and not having a brother, Namrata always tried to be a son to her parents. It was after her academics that she understood the true power of a woman entrepreneur. She started working towards her vision to build an empire through which she could take care of many such parents who don't have children/son, or stay alone.

Being a Company Secretary, Namrata always had an option to join big companies at a good salary and live a lavish life. But this was not in tune with her vision. She believes that entrepreneurs have got the power to change the world by solving various problems.

Having a secretarial and legal background, she decided to help young entrepreneurs and startups in keeping their company well complied in all aspects, so that startups can focus on core concepts of their business and grow. Thus, her mission is to give the best legal-financial-secretarial services to startups and normal business houses and help them connect with investors for funding.

Failures and successes for Namrata are a part and parcel of her journey. At a young age she tasted success in her job, being a star performer in the office. However she also realised that a 9-5 job cannot fulfill her dreams and so she quit. She started Acculegal, which is a great success. She also successfully started corporate professional classes for economically backward section of society.

She also tried setting up an academy for Kathak, but failed due to improper time management and lack of investments.

Namrata believes failures and struggles are a part of the journey. Each day comes with a new struggle, especially when running a startup. That's where you learn, step by step. Failures have taught her that there is no shortcut to success. The more you get involved in the process and enjoy the journey, the better the results would be. The approach is to have faith, be grounded and remember what didn't work out and what did.

Her first advice to all startups is to start wisely. A successful startup gives a positive impact to the ecosystem.

As a corporate secretarial expert, she highly recommends spending a good amount of time evaluating your idea and doing idea validation. Secondly, never try to walk on someone else's footprints. Each and every startup and entrepreneur have their own journey, thought process, vision, struggle and success story. Keep hustling and never settle before you achieve your vision. It is also critical to always look to give back to society.

Namrata's inspiring advice to all women entrepreneurs is "Just Do It". There are many factors that could stop a woman from starting up - society, family, relationships, looks, trends, fashion, size, shape, beauty, age, marriage, etc. All are important, but not as much as YOU, she feels. Hold a vision, prioritize yourself and start achieving the vision. Everything will come along as you focus on developing your own journey.

Namrata feels not having a son doesn't make parents weak, but having a daughter surely makes them stronger.

Mantra for Success: The only thing that can help you win over all the evils is YOU. So make yourself the most valuable one as you have the power to achieve anything and everything. Just don't stop.

About Ms. Chandni Khan

Chandni Khan is an activist and editor working for the welfare of street children in different parts of India. She founded the NGO, Voice of Slum (VOS) along with Dev Pratap Singh. She was the editor of the newspaper Balaknama, which means "voice of children", published in New Delhi. She is also called Chandni Di, the word *di* meaning "Elder Sister".

MY STORY

Can you believe that a ragpicker can run an organization? Can you believe that once a drug addict can now support slum kids in their education? But these have happened. Two children who were rag pickers in their childhood and had a tough life initiated an organization to help and support slum kids. Here is the story of my life.

At just five years, I lost my father and started picking garbage to earn a living in Delhi. You cannot even imagine the plight of a little girl who did rag picking at such a small age. I even sold flowers at the traffic signals. I was even accused of stealing and put in jail by the police. But I did not stop here. There was no home for me and life was spent at the bus stand. Some volunteers from an organisation used to come and teach the kids. There, I came in contact with the organisation that worked for slum kids. I took time off from work and started studying. That was the spirit of a young kid!

During this, I learnt about child's rights. I then started helping other kids like her whom the police locked up behind bars. The organisation appreciated my initiative. I was then associated with a venture known as 'Badhte Kadam'. I was appointed as district president and given the duty of working for the poor and slum kids. For my efforts over eight years, I got promoted from district head to National Secretary of the organisation.

I even became the reporter and editor of a newspaper 'Balaknama'. I worked in four districts and directly connected with 10,000 street children - fought for their education, rights and skills. Not just Indian kids, I also worked for children from South Asia and NCPRC.

I was awarded the Karmaveer Chakra Award Scholarship. At 18 years of age, I joined the Birla Group with a handsome salary in hand. But that did not satisfy me and came back to where I started from.

I started selling corn at the lorry. I always wanted to work for the street children. I then made a team who came from the slums and had the desire to help street kids.

Hardships of life: Story of Dev

At the age of eleven, a kid left his home with just Rs. 130. The boy was Dev who reached Gwalior station and started rag picking. Unfortunately, he got involved in stealing small things and drug addiction. Later, he started working as a waiter in a small hotel. He used to learn some words in English language from the guests who visited the hotel.

One of the guests gave him a chance to work as a waiter in a restaurant in Goa. Later, he was offered the job of territory sales manager by a company. Life was going good for Dev. But since nothing is permanent, so weren't Dev's good days. The news of his mother's death in an accident came as a shock to him. He was devastated. He now had no meaning in life. He again started taking drugs.

One day, we met and we instantly decided to set a team of people who were slum kids and wished to work for them. He had a dream to help kids selling flowers and other things at the footpath and those who begged at the traffic signals. He wanted to bring the light of education into their lives, enabling them to earn a living. Today, he is teaching 370+ poor slum kids and enlightening their lives with new hope.

Voice of Slum

On January 15, 2015, Voice of Slum was created. But the idea was not enough to help the street children. Dev and I went through a lot of hardships. We had a dream, but no resources. We did not have sufficient funds. Initially, we had only Rs. 6,000, of which Rs. 4000 was used to mortgage the laptop and only Rs. 2000 was left for our livelihood. We even ate 'Panipuri' to satisfy our hunger. Despite the hardships, we did not give up.

One day we posted a unique request on Facebook asking people to donate only Re. 1. To our surprise, we received Rs. 6,000 in just two hours. We were even noticed by some entrepreneurs who came forward to help us. Voice of Slum (VOS) got registered in 2018 through a lot of hardships.

VOS is a unique entity formed by two people who once were street kids. VOS not only educates children, but also helps them be part of the mainstream to lead a life of dignity. The organisation prepares and educates kids, enabling them to earn their livelihood once they are adults. We are working with determination and enthusiasm to support the street kids.

My Mantra for Success can be best expressed in Hindi:

जब दो कूड़ा बीनने वाले बच्चे ये सब कर सकते है, तो कोई भी कुछ भी कर सकता है, बस जरुरत है एक पहल की!

MS. NEETY GUPTA

PROPRIETOR
NEETY BUILDCON/
HEALING VIBES BY NEETY

About Ms. Neety Gupta

I am a hard-core Punjabi girl, born and brought up in Delhi. I received my education at leading schools in Delhi - Cambridge School and Air Force Golden Jubilee Institute. Being a commerce student, I followed a bachelor's and Masters at the prestigious Delhi University.

MY STORY

I believe I am a woman of strength, always seeing positivity in everything. At 44, I'm a blessed woman. By the grace of God, despite the challenge's life threw at me, I made sure to get the best out of my life. A post graduate in commerce, I started my life as a front desk representative at a leading school, soon after my wedding to my teenage love Rajesh, my 3 years senior in college. whom I married four years hence, I was all of 21 then. We are blessed with two kids, who are 21 and 18 respectively. Hard work led me through, and today I love to not only manage my home well, but also head my construction company. Our company builds ready-to-move luxury homes. I have been running my online fabric business as a wholesaler for the last eight years. Anokhi - the clothing rack supplies fabrics to boutiques across India and abroad too.

Though I was ambitious and studious, life had its own script. Soon Rajesh was out of work, I took up a job at one of the leading schools, The Shri Ram School for just Rs. 4500, as a front desk executive. It was a new experience, each day was a challenge. But all these years I have mustered the courage to face all the politics and challenges that came my way.

Before leaving home, I was expected to complete a few tasks as a new daughter-in-law. In the office, as a junior, I had to work my way through many challenges. Our son was born in 1999. Motherhood changed my life. My home became my world. In 2001, our daughter was born. By now, my husband had successfully taken over the responsibility of the family and was growing his logistics business.

I continued to be a homemaker for fifteen long years. In 2013, I decided to unleash my own ambitions.

Online business was a growing platform, I decided to play a game. With Rs. 12,000 from my mother-in-law, I bought eight suits, made a Facebook page by the name "Anokhi - the clothing Rack" and started off. Soon, the lot got sold. I reinvested and my stock of fabrics was selling like hot cakes. I only bought quality and trendy stuff. I made a broadcast list on my WhatsApp. Orders poured in every minute. I was overbooked.

But suddenly one day I lost my mother-in-law and sister-in-law in an accident. My family was devastated. I decided to take a sabbatical as my family needed me more. My husband was heartbroken. For three years, I worked only at remedial actions, putting my family together and keeping everyone united in the hour of need. My husband had a plot of land on which we decided to construct, I decided to build it and worked day and night.

Dealing with the labour, getting materials and finishing the building was a task. While my husband at times was busy in his import business, I was the face of the construction company. The site was impeccably planned by our guru and renowned architect, Shri SK Sareen. It turned out to be a beautiful project, Vastu-Perfect and well planned. It had a basement plus stilt and three floors, lift, Italian kitchen, with most modern amenities. The project was sold in just fifteen days. I bought another piece of land from my savings, after repaying the loans, thus gearing up for expansion.

Today when I look back, I feel blessed to be a woman entrepreneur. I have the full support of my husband who plans and still gets projects started. We are grateful for the blessings of our Guru and parents. I believe that no matter what goes on, the show must go on. Also remember to involve the presence of God in everything you do.

My Mantra for success: Count your blessings, pray each day. Surrender to God's will, he is the best judge.

About Ms. Namita Shah

Namita Shah is the co-founder of Presolv360, a legaltech company focused on out-of-court civil dispute resolutions. She is a CA (gold medalist), CPA and LLB. She has also studied cybercrime management from the 'Asian School of Cyber Laws'. Namita has been recognized among the Top 60 'Women Transforming India, 2018' initiative by the Government of India. She recently graduated (top 5) from the 'Women Entrepreneurship and Empowerment Foundation', run in association with Niti Aayog and IIT, and has also received a grant from the government for furthering her work).

MY STORY

If there is one thing I've learnt as a student, as a working professional, as an entrepreneur, and as a woman, it is that if we don't fail enough, we aren't aiming high enough. Let me show you how I have come to this conclusion. We all know that there is this one child in every family, in every class, which is considered stupid as he/she keeps asking questions and even questioning the simplest of things. I was that kid. In fact, I am still that kid. Today, that very kid in me is finding answers to some of the most complex problems in the legal ecosystem of our country.

I remember being diagnosed with a life-threatening disease when I was in Grade 9. I was bedridden for most of the year. I missed out on all the fun of the best years of school life. It was a tremendous blow, physically and mentally. Medicines, a miracle and prayers saved me. That's when I decided, I will live my 10th grade doubly well and make up for the missed time.

I attended every event, every competition, did literally everything I was thus far uncomfortable with and that's when I learnt some invaluable lessons, like dreaming big (even unrealistic almost), being fearless, communication skills, networking, time management. Today, the entrepreneur in me is thankful for falling ill. Without it, I'd never have expanded my horizons.

After my Std 10 results, when I decided to opt for the commerce stream and pursue chartered accountancy, I still remember my physics professor calling me and telling me that, 'Chartered Accountants only book chartered planes for those who succeed in life, and only those who take science succeed'. I was pegged to fail even before I started, and this hit me hard. But this incident also motivated me. I realised that some paths, especially like entrepreneurship, are a lonely road to tread upon. I learnt how to be my biggest cheerleader, and more so, the importance of this. Learning this has helped me make it through some of my toughest moments.

As soon as I turned 18, I traded my college life for a full-time role at an MNC and CA classes. While I saw others bunking classes and chilling, I saw myself taking notes and attending office for four years. While others had friends and dinners, I had presentations and training. Often, I found myself questioning my choices. Was the trade-off worth it? When I look back now, the answer is clear - those four years translated into a gold medal, a feat few have achieved in the CA world. More importantly, I learn the power of unshakeable faith and perseverance. What dedication, commitment and unwavering focus can lead to. These are the same principles that we apply every day in our organisation as well. The Return On Investment (ROI) is fantastic!

I still remember that sunny Monday morning when I walked into my boss' office and submitted my resignation. I suddenly quit my job without having my next steps charted out. It wasn't exactly in the spur of the moment, but it definitely wasn't planned to the T. My family, friends, peers questioned my mental abilities and repeatedly told me it was an insane decision. When I look back now, yes it was insane - Insanely good, because it led me to co-found Presolv360, a legaltech startup that is bringing dispute resolution to our fingertips, all of it using out-of-court mechanisms

It took us sixteen months to simply understand the problem and chart out a viable and effective solution. We spent those months researching, surveying, experimenting, brainstorming – without a single rupee of inflow. From a salary of a few lacs to no income for almost two years was quite an experience. It got worse. We thought we made it when a corporate committed to our solutions while we were still at a development stage. We went all out, we built an end-to-end dispute resolution software, spending every minute and every rupee in our bank account on it. Quite literally, we went all out. And when we were done, the corporate backed out. We were broke, coupled with broken spirits. I felt the same way as I did when I was diagnosed with the disease way back in Grade 9. I felt like I was dying. But that's the thing about hitting rock bottom. There's only one way to go from there – and that's upwards.

Today, I'm blessed to be working with some of India's finest corporates and dispute resolution experts.

Had it not been for all of my failures, I wouldn't be here. Success is nothing but an accumulation of failures, bouncing from one failure to another, without losing enthusiasm. And if we don't fail enough, we aren't aiming high enough.

Entrepreneurship is everything hard: lonely days, no safety nets, recurring bills, uncertain outcomes, market fluctuations, and the list simply goes on. But when you see that one satisfied customer, that one impact story which you made happen, that one 5-star review, it all seems worth it. It is a road filled with hard work and faith, at every step.

Here's my checklist for anyone who wants to choose entrepreneurship:

- Why? Because you want to solve a problem
- Is there a problem to be solved?
- Are at least 100 people you know looking for a solution?
- Is the general public looking for a solution?
- Can you make more money than you will need to burn?
- Are you passionate about it?
- Can you give up on outings, vacations, weddings, parties, etc. for the next 10 years?
- If everything was unlimited, is this what you would do?
- If you answered 'yes' to all of the above, what are you waiting for?

Being an entrepreneur is hard, but being a woman entrepreneur is unquestionably harder. This is because we have to battle not only challenges, but also perceptions, and preconceived notions too. But that's the thing with us women, we aren't ordinary humans. We are extraordinary humans. Nature has blessed us with that 'extra' and when we put our hearts and minds to something, nothing can stop us.

We all have that 'wonder woman' inside of us. All we have to do is give ourselves a chance. Have a little faith in our dreams and our abilities, and the world can be ours. There are many organisations today that are supporting women entrepreneurs, including NITI Aayog, Billennium Divas, private funds that support only women-led startups.

Believe me when I tell you it has never been a better time in the history of humanity to be a woman, especially a woman entrepreneur in India. Simply say YES to yourself. Later, when you look back, you will know it was the best decision you made for yourself.

My Mantra for Success: If you don't fail enough, you aren't aiming high enough.

DR. SANDHYA MAYENKAR

FOUNDER
SKM INSTITUTE OF CULINARY ARTS,
KINI SUPERMARKET, SKM ENTERPRISES,
SKM ASHA FOUNDATION

About Dr. Sandhya Mayenkar

Dr. Sandhya Kini Mayenkar is an epitome and a true example of women empowerment in Goa. She is the founder of Skm Institute of Culinary Arts, Skm Enterprises and Kini Supermarket. She is also the Goa State President of Women Power Society In India and Goa State President of Aesthetic International Council for Progressive Women.

MY STORY

Having trained more than 5000 women across Goa in Culinary arts and guided them into business and self-sustenance, I had also carved a niche for myself as a Successful Women Entrepreneur of the Year at various state, national and international events. I was also conferred the Title of The Honorary Doctorate for Excellence in Culinary Education and Women Empowerment at the All India Achievers Conference, New Delhi.

I have made a name for myself in fine arts too and have been a Freelance Painter by passion. I have been part of various arts exhibitions at national and international events in India and abroad. I have been travelling in and around Goa training housewives and rural women in self-help groups to enable them sell homemade stuff and get orders from home for food and bakery items. I also visit schools and train children in similar areas. Women from Goa as well as nearby states travel all the way to attend my workshops. This has been my effort for the past six years.

I have so far streamlined seventy courses and trained more than 5,000 students. Women learn skills like cooking, baking, making natural and organic cosmetics, handmade soaps and other beauty products, candle making, agarbattis, etc. It makes her happy to see many women and homemakers starting their food and other business after getting trained in my institute. I also provide guidance to small startups through her contacts to obtain various licenses and loans as well. What started as a passion for cooking and art went on to become my profession.

With my father's support and guidance, I also ventured into the supermarket business and opened up a 2,500 square metres superstore. Since then, there has been no looking back. Each day is a learning experience by itself. From being a fresher in this line to becoming one of the highest rated supermarkets in Panjim has been very satisfying. Through this venture, I am also trying to provide employment opportunities to youngsters from nearby areas. I am also an active Red Cross Society Covid19 member. In 2018, I also initiated a major Kerala Relief Fund, in association with the Goa Legal Aids Cell to collect relief materials for the flood victims. I have also been part of many cookery and bakery shows. I have also been invited as a judge for many women related events.

I have received the Achievers Award, the Incredible Goa Award for Excellence In Culinary Arts, The National Excellence Award, Rashtriya Swarnim Hind Puraskar, Incredible Art & Literature Award for Social Welfare, Naari Gaurav Samman, Youth World Indian Icon Award, Inspiring Women of Excellence, the Incredible Goa Award 2019, Nari Shakti Samman, India Star Icon, The Business Mint Award, The National Women Excellence Award, Elite Face of the Year, Goa State Brand Leadership Award, Outstanding Achievement Award conferred by Woman TV, Kala Samman Puraskar, and Guru Dronacharya Award for my contributions towards women empowerment in Goa. I was also crowned Brand Ambassador for International Pride Women by Kalakaar Foundation in 2019.

My Mantra For Success: My story is very simple and I take pride in my work. The recognition I get is a morale booster for me as well as other small town women like me, who want to stand up on their own feet, rise out of their homes to build a better life.

MY STORY

I am a software developer turned entrepreneur. I was into IT for three years before I decided to do something of my own. After leaving my corporate job, I started working for my venture Chai Network, a food and beverage startup.

It is a tea delivery chain with the aim of organising an otherwise unorganised tea market of India. We have a concept called chai for corporates - adding fuel to the workforce. We were among the top three startups of Madhya Pradesh at the i4 summit held in Bhopal.

Chai Network is a food & beverage company with prime focus on innovating solutions to deliver Chai and healthy between-the-meals food to corporate clients and educational institutions. Chai Network, as a brand, stands for delivering healthy and hygienic chai and snacks to our customers. We are focusing on creating new, innovative food designs to make chai and snacks healthier for daily consumption. After all, chai is life for many people.

We started on May 5, 2018 and got the company registered in September 2018. Chai Network started when my love for chai wasn't reciprocated by the machine-made chai in the office. I believe machine- made chai can never substitute our traditionally made chai. I channelled my interest in Ayurveda into designing food which is healthy and light on the pocket.

Success Stories

I have two dark kitchens (cloud kitchens). Over 15 corporates have subscribed for our tea subscription model. We are now delivering over 500 cups of tea daily from desk to desk. In 2019, we delivered one lac cups of tea. We wish to open 10 cloud kitchens near corporate areas and some public premium chai outlets in Indore.

As young female entrepreneurs we go through many challenges. One day a man in his early thirties, who owns a similar business as I do, came to my cloud kitchen unannounced. He had the audacity to ask me to stop serving clients because they were his clients before (and they chose my services as he was providing poor quality tea and neglecting his clients' needs). He even threatened me with dire consequences.

Entrepreneurship can be hard for female entrepreneurs and incidents like these can affect your morale. But my advice to young entrepreneurs is never give up, fight the odds. When your venture is nascent, there will be issues. In India, being a female leader comes with its own set of pros and cons. When you are dealing with blue collar workers, the challenges are unique.

Sometimes you have to let go of people who are not willing to work. Some may leave you at a crucial stage and leave you on the lurch. There was a time when for 15 days I made chai for my clients and delivered from desk to desk, as I had to keep the show running.

I took many risks. But it all seems worthy now. In May 2019 we got selected for incubation under

Atal Innovation Mission, Govt of India, where we have a food design studio for Ayurveda-based tea and snacks at Atal Innovation Center, Prestige College, Indore.

I am lucky to have supportive parents who have to put up with opinions like why she quit her IT job to sell chai. My co-founder too is supportive of my business decisions and gives me strength. Owning a business is never easy. Your venture requires your 200 per cent. My advice is never give up, keep growing and learning.

Our Future Plans

We want to expand our network of cloud kitchens to 100 in the next two years. We are exploring setting up public outlets. The whole mantra is to look at it like a network - connect the entire nation through chai. The idea of connecting India through our chai is indeed a lifelong commitment. We want to be seen as a food networking partner. Lots to be done and our goals are set.

Given the covid situation, we have decided to give back to society by launching our immunity boosting herbal tea blends label.

My Mantra For Success: Everyone will tell you to grow fast, acquire funding. I feel success is about building a sustainable business and working for something you believe in and love doing. Focus on building a brand which people can trust and never give up.

About Dr. Anubha Singhai

Dr. Anubha has completed her Masters in Cardio-Pulmonary Physiotherapy. She has an experience of thirteen years in both clinical and academic fields. She is the Editor-In-Chief of PHYSIOTIMES magazine, India's first magazine for, of and by physiotherapists. She is also the Director of PhysiQure - a chain of advanced physiotherapy clinics in Bhopal.

MY STORY

From A Physio To An Entrepreneur

I started with a focused vision to uncover the potential of physiotherapy in the Indian healthcare system. Getting together with physiotherapists and developing a world where it is easy for a physiotherapist to be with the patient even after they have gone home is what I wanted to do.

The best part of my story is the support I got from my parents and husband Anant, whom I met 20 years back at the physiotherapy college. After completing my bachelor's degree in physiotherapy, we got admission in a post graduate college in Meerut and started our careers as teachers. Then we travelled to Burhanpur and Indore. We came to Bhopal when Anant got into a government job with the Government Homeopathic Hospital, while I joined Rajiv Gandhi College and Peoples University as an Associate Professor in Physiotherapy, before joining Bansal Hospital as a clinician.

The urge to do something different and 'not settling with just what you get' made me turn into an entrepreneur. I started Physiodesk.- an exercise prescription software with the help and support of my husband. Doing something different took most of my time. Balancing it by taking care of my son and family wasn't easy.

My varied experience of 13 years taught me that nothing can be better than being your own Boss. The insecurities of your colleagues and bosses' priorities make it difficult for you to grow until you have someone to trust you completely.

The Turning Point

After working for colleges, universities, hospitals, clinics and also learning from the experience of working for Physiodesk, we got an opportunity to Acquire PHYSIOTIMES - India's first physiotherapy magazine. For that, we got an initial seed fund from Mr. Pradeep Karambelkar, Director, Vision Advisory. The technical team of Physiodesk wasn't very supportive and that I would say was a failure in my journey. But failures are the stepping stones to success. I learnt that choosing the right partner is critical.

I was always inclined towards sharing knowledge, so PHYSIOTIMES was the correct platform for me as I could connect to readers and authors across the globe. Many people told me that in a technology-driven era, selling a magazine won't be easy. But if there is a will, there is a way. With just four freshers, I took up the new responsibility to begin a new chapter. The magazine, which was closed for more than a year had to be revived, which included:

- Pitching for advertisers and for new subscribers
- Approaching celebrities to add more value to the product
- Motivate the budding physios to read and explore more.

We worked day and night within six months, and we were back in business. It was more of setting your own standards and striving hard to achieve it. I was overwhelmed when Ankita Raina, Bhaichung Bhutia, PT Usha and Abhinav Bindra agreed to share their stories. It gave me confidence that I can do better. In less than six months, we reached 500+ subscribers and got advertisements from international institutes.

We entered the clinical service sector with a technology-driven approach. With the help of Mr. Pradeep Karambelkar, we developed a new entity and founded Phycon Healthcare Private Limited.

Phycon Healthcare Private Limited was incorporated in March 2019 with a vision to provide physiotherapy for the masses and serve people. We started with a single clinic and developed software to manage and standardise the clinical practice of physiotherapy. Within four months of incorporation, Phycon Healthcare acquired PHYSIOTIMES.

After this acquisition, Phycon Healthcare started an investment campaign for their dream project to set up a chain of physiotherapy clinics. Within six months of this campaign, Phycon Healthcare was able to raise 1 Crore from Series A Fund and founded a joint venture PhysiQure Healthcare Private Limited. PhysiQure's team has well qualified and trained physiotherapists in Bhopal. We choose the best protocol-led treatment plan which will make the recovery a positive and painless process. The use of technology in physiotherapy will make it reachable and accessible to all with ease. Technology will enable us to scale and provide a unified and quality solution to all.

The lockdown has not limited us. We are a team of innovative, empathetic, exemplary healthcare professionals who are driven by passion, inspiration and performance as we care for our clients from every age, stage and walk of life. We provide the most advanced and best physiotherapy services that are affordable and approachable. Our mission is to make physiotherapy approachable and affordable for all.

I follow the rules of chess and one of them is to create backups. PhysiQure Healthcare is working hard to achieve that. From two people, we have grown to 23 which itself is very motivating. Process and execution are the keys to success. We are going phase wise to establish our clinics. In the first phase, we have planned for ten clinics in MP.

The journey has been fulfilling though not easy. Work-life balance is the key and hard work pays.

As Colin Powell said: "There are no secrets to success. It is the result of preparation, hard work and learning from failure."

My advice to startups is to dream bigger and believe in themselves. Only then they'll be able to make others believe in them. Never be afraid to try new things, even if others find them odd.

My advice to women entrepreneurs is to take a moment and look back. You must have talents that made you happy and your parents proud. Don't accept that marriage and kids will change everything. Don't limit your energies to the kitchen and household. You can do much more. Just believe in your dreams and don't feel bad when you see other women making more dishes. You are taking much more pains to balance your life and work - two dishes less will do.

Today, I am balancing a lot of things – my family, son, magazine, new project of PhysiQure, discussing the importance of physiotherapy on different public platforms like Bansal News, social media, etc. I believe we must stay hungry and stay foolish.

My Mantra For Success: Always put your 100 percent in whatever you do.

About Ms. Ivy Manohara

With a BSc & a MSc in Environmental science and Environmental management I went on to do an Management Program on Entrepreneurship from IIM Bangalore. Leveraging a couple of decades of professional experience in Advanced Spatial Technology, Program and Project Management, Education, Environmental Sciences, Training and Communication. I have spent time in, and absorbed the experiences of the lean-mean, highly effective, corporate companies, the sluggish public sector, the creative film and production houses, precision-based manufacturing industries, scientific laboratories, schools and colleges, large international non-profit organizations and charities. I have also been fortunate to have had a lot of remarkable opportunities and experiences while travelling the world, and working with extremely talented and smart people around the globe.

MY STORY

I come from an average, middle-class family in Bangalore. My large family is filled with only teachers and government employees. So a good college education followed by becoming a teacher or government employee was always expected of me. And hence, I became a teacher, but for the first three years of my career only. Thereafter, I moved on to a corporate job in an international mining company. My family was not happy that I quit teaching. For many young women, teaching is an ideal profession, since it allows you to focus on your family once you get married.

I had moved into the technical domain of mining and exploration. By virtue of my job, I had to travel a lot and was fortunate enough to travel around the world. My family was further alarmed that I was not quite "settling down". Instead, I led an extremely busy corporate life. In 2006, much to their relief, I got married to an IT engineer. Now both of us were busy and things were progressing on an even keel…… but life had other plans!

In the middle of my corporate career, the 2008 recession struck hard and both of us lost our jobs. Burdened with heavy debt, my husband and I were forced to do odd jobs. Four years of unemployment took a toll on us. But life had a silver lining.

It was during this time that we came up with the idea of Filmapia. I co-founded Filmapia along with my husband. I was chosen as one of the 10,000 women by Goldman Sachs Programme and incubated at IIM-B for three months in 2019. I was also awarded the 'Digital Women Awards' in the Market Disruption category in 2019.

An Accidental Entrepreneur

I had a lot of time during the four years of unemployment. A movie and travel buff, I watched a lot of movies on DVDs. While watching these movies, I would often wonder where these movies were shot. There was not much information on the Internet and hence I decided to find out and put it on the Internet for people like me. I sought my husband's help to make a small website where I would research and put location information about movies. I would continuously watch movies and keep adding them to the website which became popular with a lot of movie and travel buffs.

Then a strange thing started happening. I started getting enquiries from Filmmakers to help them shoot at the different locations that were on the website. While researching on this line of enquiry we got to know more about the over 120-year-old chaotic and unorganised film locations market. My husband and I decided to do our bit in trying to bridge the gap by bringing in technology and processes, which were our strengths.

Initially, I worked on small projects which involved minimal research and simple permissions and arrangements for shootings. But soon I realised that I had no clue about how the film industry worked.

Meanwhile, the recession lifted and we got back to our corporate careers. However, the idea of Filmapia was still there in our minds. To get some practical experience, we often travelled to Mumbai and Chennai to talk to industry experts and watch shoots. All this while holding highly-demanding IT jobs. We continued this for almost eight years and I loved every minute of it.

In 2017, we took the bold decision of quitting our jobs to take up Filmapia as a business full-time. Our families were extremely annoyed at our decision. They thought we had gone insane to quit high-paying corporate jobs to get into the infamous film industry. But we went ahead nevertheless, testing our fate and betting on our passion.

Now, what is Filmapia. Film location hunting is one of the most painful, unpredictable and expensive tasks in filmmaking. Filmapia solves this problem at every level. We democratise location hunting, bringing in transparency and saving costs of time and money up to 5X or more. We built Filmapia as an online platform for film shooting locations (www.filmapia.com). We realised that it was and still is one of its kind venture in India.

To give an analogy, we are like AirBnB for film locations. We partner with countries, cities, villages, etc for shootings in their destinations. We showcase them and their policies to filmmakers across the country and facilitate shootings. In several instances, we have had foreign productions reach out to us to shoot in India and we have facilitated those successfully too. I run research & development and sales for Filmapia, and collaborate with clients across India and in a few other countries.

In its three years of business, Filmapia has provided locations for around 200+ feature films, advertisements, TV serials, corporate and digital videos, documentaries, photoshoots and events across different cities in India. We have also worked across the spectrum, from student short film makers to big names like Google, Facebook, and big film production banners.

Successes and Failures

My initial journey was filled with failures. Being from a technology background, with no connections in the film industry, we had to learn everything that was a 'film' from the ground up - from procuring location permissions to being the "spot boys" during a film shoot to building a business…all this the hard way.

Once we managed to source a very difficult location for a film director. He was so pleased with our work that he promised to introduce us to all the big directors in the industry. He seemed so well connected that when he said he would pay us the location fees at the end of the shoot, we did not mind. During the shoot, the film team damaged property and broke a lot of rules. At the end of the shoot, the director disappeared without paying us the money. Not only did we lose money, but we also lost credibility with the location.

Recently, we had a TV serial shoot at a palatial house. Due to a communication lapse on our side, the location owner had to forcibly remove the sets erected by the film team. The reasons themselves were complicated, so we offered to compensate for the loss.

We had some glorious successes too.

When we were planning the music launch for the movie 'Lucknow Central' in 2018, the producers wanted to release it in Yerawada Jail in Pune. While having entertainment shows is easy in Tihar Jail, Yerawada is a strict no-zone for such activities. Even the most competent line producers in Bollywood failed to arrange this event. We managed to get it done through sheer persistence. It took us 40 days of consistent hard work with the Maharashtra Prisons officials. What followed was a grand event in the presence of 5,000+ prisoners. Even Farhan Akthar was full of praise for us.

We are working with a photographer from Finland who is creating a documentary and photo exhibition of rags-to-riches billionaires across the world. Several people have tried getting interviews with these important people, but have failed. However we have managed to do that in several countries and got some excellent documentary material via interviews and photoshoots with each billionaire. It makes us feel proud of our work when we get praise from him.

We celebrate our successes and lose sleep over our failures. But somehow there is a die-hard optimism and belief in me that each failure is another brick in making our company resilient and shock-proof. With every mistake we made, we went back to the drawing board, reflected on our mistakes and set up a process to plug the gap. Failure has taught me more than success ever has.

My Advice to Women Entrepreneurs

It is a good time to be a woman entrepreneur. Women have the inherent strength and traits that are needed to build a business with a strong foundation. Pioneers such as Billennium Divas are giving the required push to get more women to step up, step out and dare to walk the untrodden path. If you find yourself in a male-dominated industry, don't be afraid.

As a woman entrepreneur, if you are confident, put forth the right message consistently and show that you mean business. Even those who discriminate will eventually toe the line. The world is evolving and so are people's perceptions.

Advice for Startups

If you have a dream, a passion, hold on to it. The world will open doors for you. When you do establish your idea as a business, strive for quality and excellence, not money. Serve to improve it every day with honest effort. The money will come sooner or later. Let money not be your goal. As the entrepreneurial journey continues, I learn every single day, and I am having the time of my life.

My Mantra for Success: Dream Big. Work Hard. Be Patient.

MS. SUVARNA BHAT

FOUNDER & CEO
BHOOMIPUTRI BY KADAMBA

About Ms. Suvarna Bhat

Post graduate in Journalism and Mass Communication from Karnataka University, Dharwad, Karnataka. I have 20 years of professional experience as a freelancer, Social Entrepreneur. I have associated with many like minded individuals to empower women and make their living a better place by associating with social causes such as child and women empowerment, skill development, green initiative like tree plantation drive etc. I am a Freelancer and Social Entrepreneur, Founder CEO, Bhoomiputri an initiative by Kadamba, Founder Director at Inquisite Innovations Pvt. Ltd.

MY STORY

Malenadu is a place in coastal Karnataka which is situated in the western ghats. The literal meaning of Malenadu is Hilly region. Born and brought up in Malenadu, I had my education in places all around Karnataka. Trained in Journalism from Karnataka University, I pursued journalism during my initial career days. Distant Hyderabad became my KaryaKshetra after marriage.

I had my larger interests in mind and wanted to be independent. This craving led to my first entrepreneurial venture in the form of Pre-School "Akshara" and later to one of the prominent brands of Ayurveda "ShathayuAyrveda" franchise.

Any business or venture will find success provided the person at the helm of affairs has sincerity and zeal to succeed. I prepared well at the drawing board and meticulously implemented the strategies for my ventures.

The root cause of modern-day health issues are lifestyle related. I believe we must fine tune the way we live with the help of systems like Aurveda and holistic living. Shathayu Ayurveda was an ideal venture for me for being an entrepreneur and also living the dream of holistic living.

Malenadu is also known for its green forest cover. People from the region are plant lovers and Suvarna is no different. The love for plants and nature brought her close to the Telangana government's wonderful initiative 'Harith Haram'. I took active participation in Harith Haram and organised events for plantations across Hyderabad with like-minded people. The country can prosper if only if balance is maintained between development and respect for nature.

My commitment to developing a better society made me work in the field of affordable housing, life assessment and extension of building and structures.

Thus my venture Inquisite Innovation LLP took birth. Safety of every human being is paramount. The buildings and structures also need inspection, repair and assessment.

Training the future generations for them to take up the challenges of life is very important. So people should share their experiences. With social media playing a critical role in every field, we can learn faster. So, I started a web portal Goalbrew.com, where one can narrate a story to inspire and relive the moments. The stories range from life's experiences to technical stuff.

Birth of Bhoomiputra: The humble women farmers whom I have come across since my childhood are the biggest influence on my life. Without expecting anything in return, a women farmer performs her farm duties, takes care of the family and children. All she expects is to make life easier for herself and her family. I have read somewhere that "there is nothing which cannot be achieved in life if it doesn't matter who gets the credit". A women farmer is a perfect example for this. Hence the Bhoomiputris of India are the ones who influence me to do my bit, however little it may be. "Bhoomiputri", a unique platform for women farmers an initiative by Kadamba took birth which aims to be active in the agri sector and in service of farmers. Through the Bhoomiputri initiative, we aim to bridge this gap and contribute our bit in supporting the farmers and society as a whole.

I take pride in dealing with women-centric issues. Improving women's participation and productivity in the economy improves the overall well-being of communities and the society. This requires accounting for and addressing the legal, socio-cultural and political barriers that keep many women and girls from participating fully in their economies and societies. By engaging and investing in women's organisations, the voices of women and girls can be amplified.

If one feels that there will only be success, that is not reality. Failures provide lessons success cannot. After every failure, an intelligent person does root cause analysis of that failure. The analysis teaches us what we are not supposed to do and the better methods one must employ.

I tasted failure too. The Akshara School, which was successful initially, did not continue to grow as volume also plays an important role. Corporate schools invest huge amounts of money and start big. Starting big plays an important role in the minds of parents as they feel bigger schools will contribute more to the development of their children.

Similarly, the venture "WeEmpower" was registered as a charitable trust. WeEmpower was a facilitating platform for the enterprising dreams of women right from visualisation to actualisation by creating the right ecosystem to nurture their dreams. I was Founder Director of the Trust. The vision was to empower women through self-help networking structures across the country; build women entrepreneurship from homes and nurture them to be self-made entrepreneurs. However, the venture could not stand the test of time due to partnership issues. For a venture to sustain the right kind of understanding is between the business partners.

My advice for budding entrepreneurs is to not hesitate to take risks. Never think failure means lack of capability on your part. Discuss with people who have seen the world which you are trying to explore. Do not hesitate to open up with your difficulties. Believe in yourself.

My Mantra For Success: When your presence is strongly felt, your purpose is fairly met. Reach more to serve more. Innovation is serendipity. Success doesn't necessarily come from breakthrough innovation, but from flawless execution. A great strategy alone won't win a game or a battle, the win comes from how good and effective the implementation is.

About Dr. Megha Bhatt

Dr. Megha Bhatt is a veteran with 25 years' experience in academics and 10 years in research. She holds a Masters in Botany (Mithibai College, Mumbai) and a Doctorate (Ph.D) with a workplace as SAC, ISRO, Ahmedabad. As a scientist, she has accomplished a prestigious project under the WOS-A scheme, Department of Science & Technology (DST), Government of India. Dr. Megha is currently associated with NAC (National Academic Committee) and has acted as the district, state and national evaluator in the National Children's Science Congress (NCSC) along with undertaking its teacher's training program. Dr. Bhatt has also been involved as an anchor with GUJCOST, Science City & GUBS (Gujarat University Botanical Society).

MY STORY

Since childhood, I loved teaching and always wanted to become an educator. After my post-graduation, I became a full-time lecturer in Mithibai College, Mumbai and taught in the masters' programme for five years. After marriage, I came to Ahmedabad and started studying again to pursue my Ph.D, accompanied by motherhood. Due to my husband's intra-company transfers, got shifted to the US for a few years. We took a conscious call and came back to India for good in 2009.

I came across a scheme by DST, Govt of India, for women with a break in their careers to rejoin the science stream. I had done extensive review work by referring to more than 4,000 papers and made a project proposal, presented and was chosen from 654 participants for fellowship with 26 other participants from across India. It gave an identity of a woman scientist.

Meanwhile, I kept teaching in a temporary position at the post graduate level till 2017. The subject was the newly introduced course on Climate Change and Impacts Management at Gujarat University. I was also working as a visiting faculty at Nirma and PDPU for Environmental studies. As visiting faculty, there wasn't any job security. But I still did not opt for entrepreneurship as I wanted to teach. As it is said, many inventions are accidental. Life took a twist with my initiative "SciKnowTech" which I created as a breakthrough in "Experiential Science learning" for school going kids in 2015.

Why I became an entrepreneur

Being hardcore a educationist and then a scientist, I never dreamt of turning towards entrepreneurship. But the idea came from my son and children around. Only conceptual learning or exposure to experiments/models actually was inadequate to learn science effectively.

Children knew how to do the experiments watching YouTube videos, but didn't know the why behind them. I felt I was best placed to answer those questions. Thus, with the philosophy of 'Exposure Leads To Exploration', I came up with the idea of having SciKnowTech - a breakthrough in experiential science learning, exposing children to various aspects using multiple languages of learning, audio-visual, expert's intervention, field trips, experiments, model making, creative craft work and story-telling.

Using different methods to introduce the same concept or topic definitely makes them think out-of- the-box and gain clarity too. In cities, there are either tuition classes or activity centres, but we offer a programme which is graded from Standard 2-10, not only covering theory like tuition classes, but everything else like any activity centre to give an experience.

For children to explore and innovate, I have created creative labs for all the three sciences in Ahmedabad's Satellite area. We have also designed and implemented an activity-based Maths module with the name SciKnowMath. Have started SciKnowTalk – a lecture series open and free for all to spread science in a meaningful way to the society by calling the best of subject experts to talk to children in the simplest possible language. As our tagline is Exposure Leads to Exploration, when we got exposed to the pandemic, it made us explore the new vertical of online creative offering, SciKnowNet. It's really amazing with kids associating from across India and abroad. It is so much fun combining theory, audio-visual, demonstrations and activities with household things.

The mission of my business

Experiential learning of science and maths to kids with multiple languages of learning with year-long programmes, workshops, science clubs, teacher's training and now online learning are the business modules for this endeavour. These modules are designed grade-wise, concept wise and to give actual experience using different languages of learning for kids. This method surely nurtures the attitude and develops the analytical aptitude in children for the subject of science. Our mission is to spread science in a meaningful way in the form of basics and application-based learning.

My failures and successes

I was a full-time lecturer in Mithibai College, Mumbai, for five years. The first failure I feel is being unemployed, as after getting married and coming to Ahmedabad, due to the rigid structure of the system. But I changed that to success by putting up a project proposal in DST, Govt of India, under the women scientist programme. I received a fellowship worth 26,00,000 INR and also got a beautiful identity of a Women Scientist.

Coming from a biology background, I was not tech-savvy. But during covid, I learnt to adapt. I feel you should never give up on your passion. My passion has been teaching. I converted the failure of not getting employed by universities (for various reasons which I cannot mention here) to a fantastic and one-of-its-kind initiative for children in learning science. The best part is, this initiative got me so many accolades in a short period of time.

My advice to startups

One can become an entrepreneur at any age, if one is confident about one's own expertise, subject knowledge and is creative enough to innovate. If you have an idea, understand the market need, build a fantastic team complementing one another and indulge in implementing your idea passionately.

My advice to women entrepreneurs

Believe in Yourself first and work hard in the right direction. Have Ideas, but also have the guts to implement them. Identify your business USP, your strengths and also your weaknesses. Combine your passion with compassion.

SciKnowTech started just around 4.5 years ago with seven kids at home. We have already catered to around 3,5000 kids in terms of exposing them to science experiential learning through more than 425 Workshops and over 85 teachers' training programmes.

My Mantra For Success: Exposure Leads To Exploration and Exploration to Innovation.

With her initiative SciKnowTech, she has bagged awards such as:
1. Digital Woman award in Disruption category by SheThePeople TV in association with Google
2. Gujarat Innovation Society (GIS) – Trendsetter Award for spreading science in a meaningful way
3. National Start-up and Innovation Summit (Best Start-up).
4. "Social Impact Award" by GUSEC (Gujarat University Startup and Entrepreneurship Council)
5. Udgam Women Achievers Award for Science Communication).

About Ms. Roli Pandey

I am a BE (Computer Science Engineering) – Chhattisgarh Swami Vivekananda Technical University, Raipur. An MBA from Symbiosis International University, Pune, I am also a Member of Brochure Committee, Member of Guest Lecture Committee, Member of Pan Pune Blood Donation Organizing Committee

Some of the Certifications I have acquired are Startup India Learning Program (by Invest India), Women Entrepreneurship Development Program (WEDP) under Department of Science and Technology, India, AICTE Startup Mentorship Program 2018 by MHRD and Canada India Center of Excellence, Augmented Reality by Google, Y Combinator Startup School (Batch 2019).

Accomplishments: Responsible for making Zucate a Nasscom 10000 Startup, Secured a mentor from SINE IIT Powai, from IVY Camp, Represented India in World Entrepreneurs Investment Forum, by United Nations Industrial Development Organization in Manama, Bahrain 2017, Interview by Facebook for Innovation of Zucate, Invited for LIVE interaction with the honourable Prime Minister Shri Narendra Modi for his interaction with innovative entrepreneurs across India for #InnovationkiBaatPMKeSaath, Zucate accelerated in XR Accelerator by Unity Technologies at Kerala Startup Mission in Kochi.

Awards And Achievements

➢ Wee Fellow at SINE IIT Mumbai by WEE Foundation Mentorship Program under NITI Aayog
➢ Startup Leadership Fellow 2019-2020
➢ Mentor at Institution Innovation Council at RDNC under Mumbai University).

MY STORY

Being a computer science engineering graduate from a small city Raipur and an MBA from Symbiosis, Pune, my only dream at one point like many was to get a high-paying job. While working as a Business Development Manager at a healthcare IT company, I realised that a cubicle was too small a place to take the burden of my dreams. Little did I know that for many a salary at the end of every month could be the sole point of happiness and satisfaction. While watching a bunch of employees dressed smartly and working in posh offices during my graduation days. I used to get creativity fits periodically, which were killed instantly.

Nipping creativity at its bud is unfortunately a part of corporate culture in India. I found that my batchmate from Symbiosis Dr. Moitreyee Goswami, who also happened to be my flatmate at that time back in 2013 (and still continues to be), faced the same anxiety. The grass is always greener on the other side, until you cross the fence. So, once the fence was crossed, we both just felt the urge and empowerment to quit our jobs (without the consent of our families of course) and start Enlightening Minds.

Enlightening Minds (intended to enlighten students and hence the ambitious name) was our first venture, an educational institute in the prime location of Pune. We knew nothing about starting up and hence the first thing that we did was to get 5,000 pamphlets printed. Now the problem was what to do with that large pile stacked in our home? So, we got some of them distributed through newspapers.

We still had a huge number left with us. Being shy, we were not exposed to the real world it seemed. Thus, we started going after 9 pm everyday with pamphlets and glue-gum in our bags and pasting them at every place possible, right from bus stops to park benches to a half-cut tree stump in the middle of the road. Trust me, that half-cut tree stump for some strange reason fetched us more students than any other marketing channel.

Most of the parents we asked said they saw our adverts on the tree stump, most probably to find out who on earth and for what reason would stick something to a cut tree stump. At Enlightening Minds, we have taught more than 550 students in the last six years and have seen an improvement of more than 135 per cent in our students' performance. The revenue was good and so was the profitability. Every success builds confidence to move ahead and do new things, as we are never satisfied with what we have.

In 2015, we wanted to expand Enlightening Minds to the rest of Pune, but the infrastructure cost hampered our growth. Being graduates from the healthcare sector and also having worked in the same industry, we started Integrate Haleness. It was a preventive healthcare B2B start-up. We did tie-ups with major pathology labs across India and made available our facilities in 23 cities.

We onboarded doctors, dentists, ophthalmologists, as well as mobile clinics across India. We wanted it to be big and hence also tied up with a global smart health card company as an exclusive partner. It was a HIPPA compliant card and had a chip-based system to store patient's health data. We started doing cold calls to the corporates. But in the next six months, we kept on listening to No's from the staggering 822 calls and the follow up mails we had sent.

'NO' seemed to be so common that every time we picked up the phone, it seemed the IVR system would start uttering the word to us. People (HR Managers, CEOs, and so on...) used to call and email us for meetings only to forget our names upon arrival at their offices. We failed miserably in a year's time as all our proposals got turned down because the employers didn't want to spend on employee's health back then.

We had forgotten to do our homework well. The lesson: When you study marketing management in your MBA days (and even if you don't), you better take it seriously and conduct a market research to find out whether the fancy product ideas that you come up with are worth investing the time and money by asking people whether they need it. Integrate Haleness started going down the drains by the end of 2015 and with it the burden of stress, panic attacks and periods of frustration and depression started doing the rounds with both of us.

Depression became a commonplace and routine in the beginning of 2016. But as they say, when everything falls apart in life, there opens a door that gives you hope. All this time, the only sane thing that we both did was trying to take the core business of Enlightening Minds online in the name of Zucate Minds, while working on Integrate Haleness. We had applied to various platforms and when we hit the peak of depression and were about to call entrepreneurship quits, Zucate became a NASSCOM 10000 Startup.

It seems like yesterday that we were spending our entire day thinking why it happened to us and the next day we were standing at the Bombay Stock Exchange at the Zone Startup's Office at a NASSCOM event pitching Zucate to leading investors in the country.

There has been no looking back since then. Zucate got mentors from IIT and became a part of reputed programs like Microsoft Bizspark Plus, Incubation at Symbiosis Centre for Entrepreneurship and Innovation, only start-up representation from India at United Nations' World Entrepreneurs Investment Forum 2017, Vibrant Gujarat Startup and Technology Summit and acceleration at Kerala Startup Mission, which is in collaboration with Unity Technologies.

Zucate has been the shining star in our entrepreneurial journey. Through Zucate we are trying to create an impact in India's education system. We are revolutionising the idea of self-study. We have devised an augmented reality-based solution which can read the school textbook and show it to the students in a 2D or 3D format based on the content in the book. It provides school students a real-life experience, otherwise missing in textbooks. It also offers personalisation to cater to the abilities of every student by showing adaptability in terms of content, speed and time.

Being from an orthodox family, I never got the courage to tell my family about the failure of Integrate Haleness and the inception of Zucate. The prime reason behind it was as they were already dissatisfied with my career choices, it would have only added to my troubles.

One of the most impactful achievements as well as a moment of truth came when we won the Canada India Acceleration Program, which was an exchange program between AICTE, MHRD, Government of India, Carleton University and Government of Canada. They had put up the winners' list on their website and my family came across that post the day we won. So when other winners were celebrating their victory in Delhi and went on a tour together, my co-founder and I were sitting sadly in our hotel room as I was getting a mouthful over a phone call. I was called a traitor to our family who had spoiled their name. They even blamed my co-founder for no reason.

Had it not been for my co-founder Moitreyee's support and encouragement, it wouldn't have been possible for a caterpillar like me to break the cocoon and spread my wings. Her motivation has surpassed the number of times I have faced insults. To date, not a month has gone by when my family hasn't been angry with me. This has made me realise that even though I can put a dent in the business world, I can never make some people happy and so have moved on with my choices.

My co-founder Moitreyee and I felt that entrepreneurial prick in December 2019. We thought that we should utilize the knowledge we had gained in building Zucate to help other entrepreneurs so that they could build fast and didn't have to face what we had gone through. There was no technology help and mentorship when we started. With this intention, we incepted WebbTechy, which is our technology development and digital marketing start-up, which helps other start-ups build their online presence in one sixth the time as well as at one sixth the cost. This will help them realise their dreams faster than we could do.

My entrepreneurial journey has shown me the true face of many aspects of my life. I have realised that if you don't fit into the society's definition of success, you are considered downtrodden and are treated likewise. I have also realised that we women are used to multitasking since time immemorial. We are currently riding on two horses - Zucate and WebbTechy, and trust me, the excitement has doubled, with the journey becoming even more interesting.

Entrepreneurship is like a bug. Once bitten, the impact remains and will continue to as long as you live. So, so far so good…

My Mantra for Success: The key to your true potential is within you, and you realize it when your status quo is challenged; entrepreneurship does exactly that.

About Dr. Tejal Kanwar

Dr. Tejal is a Post graduate in M.D. (Gynaecology) from K.E.M. and Wadia Hospital. International Training: Trained in Advanced Gynaecological Endoscopic Surgery, Anatomy & Virtual Reality training at the Department of Obstetrics & Gynaecology, University of Kiel, Germany. Has worked in Rajawadi and Somaiya hospital as a lecturer. Is practicing privately for the last 15 years. Has presented several papers, research work in conferences, and also helped organise seminars.

After starting Kleinetics, she received media recognition from top portals as an innovative and socially impactful business. The plaudits from Outlook Business WOW and the Billennium Divas competition in 2019 provided a great deal of encouragement as it was chosen as a top unique idea. The business was chosen in TIECON 2020 as a unique startup for a pitch session).

MY STORY

My Journey From Mom And Doctor To Fitness Entrepreneur

I joined a kickboxing fitness class, and it was the pivotal shift that changed my life forever. The activity was super energising and my stamina was at an all-time high. One day, I dragged my seven-year-old son to one of the sessions.

As a low birth weight baby, wanting to be a footballer, he used to get demotivated as he was not strong and fast enough in his school team. I knew he needed to build core strength, get better with his speed and reflexes. I wanted to see if this class could interest him.

Around the same time, as a gynaecologist, in my clinic I treated teenage girls with pre-diabetes, body image issues, PCOD, postural and muscular weaknesses. All these critical issues could be traced to lifestyle. I spent some sleepless nights wondering how I could protect my own daughter, then nine. None of the solutions I sought with sports trainers seemed designed to meet this challenge. They were doing the same thing for decades, putting kids through strict, boring exercise routines.

The existing fitness methodologies ignored the fact that the kids didn't even have basic physical literacy, since this generation has stopped playing, hopping, running, climbing and falling. Mastering ABCs of physical literacy would allow kids to move confidently and with control in a wide range of physical activity situations.

What was required was to build them into confident individuals on the playground so that they could hit the ball harder, endure hours of play, accept a loss and get back on their feet, be team players, and learn to manage their time balancing sports and academics.

The kickboxing class with my son changed everything. The trainer, a friend, Mohit Sahni was focused on fitness, learning advanced Muay Thai, certifying himself in a host of training methodologies. When my son came to the class, Mohit engaged him in playful challenges that got him interested. That moment led to flushing out an idea that could work with children. With Mohit's inputs, we put into motion experimenting a beta project in the neighbourhood, to build a new play time for the colony's kids.

My leap into entrepreneurship

My kids were now both part of their school football teams. Pardita, a friend whose child had just won a prestigious sports title, was kind in giving us a ridiculous amount of credit for the victory. As I researched around, looking for collaborators, it became clear that the methodology we were using was first of its kind. I began to see the huge impact I could have with building new fitness games and it was time to think of growing this.

The challenge was that my husband Saurabh too was in an early-stage start-up, so we would be stretching resources and risking stability. But all doubts dissipated as everyone, including my in-laws, were very supportive and encouraged me to take the plunge.

I drew on the wisdom from my medical networks to help shape the product. Meanwhile, Saurabh and his business partner Prashant brought in a lot of their start-up experience, helping me avoid the pitfalls, set up the brand, content and business models. We applied human-centered-design principles to go-to-market, and it was evident that we would be able to sell the idea only if the class was in school or near home, since parents did not prefer to travel. Kids gained in group dynamics and socially too.

My journey into the world of entrepreneurship commenced with a slow, steady approach, with no marketing. Moms were our biggest ambassadors. Even if one child liked a demo, the mother would pass the word around helping generate warm leads.

The product

Workouts are for adults. Kids need to play, so we applied the rules of entertainment to make every session interesting. We took everyday games and added physical aspects to them, measuring the kids periodically, assigning a simple-to-understand score to gauge the progress. The word Kleinetics comes from compounding 'kinetic' with the German 'kleine', meaning little. The idea is to evoke an engineered system that is built on doing small things for little people, with big outcomes.

The coaches are sports athletes, achievers in their game. The coach at Kleinetics to support themselves as they build their sports careers. This means they bring passion and playfulness along with a structured program in which they get trained by a chief coach. At the time of writing this, we are in 70 plus locations, including 25 schools. The most critical consideration for us is that within a year of hitting schools, we have been integrated within the curriculum of several schools, rather than just being an add-on class.

The Ups and Downs

Nobody said entrepreneurship is easy, but nothing can prepare you for just how challenging this journey can be. MBBS and MD are gruelling, demanding a tough work ethic. You have to work for 48 hour shifts, seeing hundreds of patients a day. And then as an obstetrician, patients can deliver any time of the day or night.

But entrepreneurship is like being in college again, learning new things while you are deep in the middle of a surgery; you are the surgeon, the nurse, the ward-boy and sometimes even the patient. The early days were a blur. My kids were young and with no office, I worked from home, having equipment in my car. The team became my extended family. Interviews, several coffees, excel sheets, prop training, brainstorming new ideas, small victories, chief coach cooking lunch for the team, dousing daily fires, farewells and lots of problem solving happened in my home. Every single morning, with my husband, our coffee ritual for four years has been to talk about work, where I pick his brains, argue and solve problems. Sometimes the discussions spill over to dinner, and the kids politely ask us to shut up.

The lowest point probably came early. We always knew that schools would provide for maximum impact and a larger number of receptive kids. I excitedly went in for the first appointment as the principal was receptive, saying their academically-oriented kids would benefit. The frustration started when we were handed over to the PT teacher. The portly gentleman blocked us saying we were no match for him. He yelled at us till we were out of the gate. The very person who should have resonated with our message the most, felt the most threatened.

Subsequently, with the blessings of encouraging parents in school PTA's who evangelised our cause, the most rewarding moment came after a demo at a school for students with learning disabilities. The school invited us to experiment for their play therapy and helped us customise the program. We saw tremendous results, and it is still one of the most satisfying centres for us, because of the joy it brings to the kids. Equally gratifying was when we trained an underprivileged girls' kabaddi team. The girls would arrive in their burqas, and transform into assertive players. I ended up hiring some of them as assistant trainers.

The Future

The world is undergoing a transformation. The mindset of parents towards preventive health is rapidly shifting towards receptiveness. Marathons, gyms and fitness centres are witnessing a substantial footfall of parents who want their children to get the required dose of workouts beyond just marks and ranks.

Are we doing enough? Not at all. We have just scratched the surface and the rest of India awaits. On many days, it feels like we are moving too slow, even as I can see that the world calls out. But there are other considerations. While it is important to be profitable so that the business can grow, I think that ventures should also be measured by the social problems that they solve.

As a woman entrepreneur, I am able to flourish with a good team of hardworking women helming the operations. We also have a national level female athlete as a core team member now. I hope to help as many women become financially independent and socially secure as possible.

I will not be satisfied till we create a world class program out of this pure 'Make in India' product that runs on the shoulders of strong women. The most visible impact will be in the male-dominated sports industry. We believe that we need to get our girls more confident to be able to have more Sanias, Sainas, Sindhus, Sakshis and Marys, Mithalis and Manikas.

My Mantra For Success: Don't merely own the idea, own the execution too and build on it.

ABOUT THE AUTHORS

Bhavesh Kothari is passionate about making a difference to women entrepreneurs through the power of learning and mentoring. Bhavesh carries over two decades of experience in sales and marketing. As Director of Billennium Divas, he is committed to inspire women entrepreneurs to conquer their limitations and showcase their incredible prowess to the world. He is a passionate mentor and is associated with various forums as a Mentor-Speaker, mentors various startups and is on the mentor board of several renowned incubators in the country. He also facilitates funding for startups via SyndiCap Venture Partners. He is a community builder and his mantra is "Build Value and the Valuation will Follow"

Bhavesh Kothari

LinkedIn Profile: https://www.linkedin.com/in/bhaveshkothari1511

Email Id: billenniumdivas@gmail.com

Hariharan Iyer started his career in research and built his journey as a journalist. Eventually, he took to his core passion - Speaking And Training. He is a celebrated Speaker, Trainer and Author with over 25 years of learning & development experience. He has authored seven other books too. Hariharan is the Founder & Chief Mentor of Hariharan's School Of Success Education (HSSE) established in 2009. He holds a unique registered trademark for the moniker 'The Enter-Trainer'.

Hariharan Iyer

LinkedIn Profile: https://www.linkedin.com/in/hariharan-iyer-the-enter-trainer-54456516

Email Id: hariharan@theentertrainer.in

www.ingramcontent.com/pod-product-compliance
Lightning Source LLC
Chambersburg PA
CBHW021544200526
45163CB00015B/1274